To: Jessie

Thank you for
God be with x.

[signature]
9-14-19

Pushing Forward: Copyright @ 2019 Hezekiah Watkins and Andrea Ledwell
First Printing.

All rights reserved. No part of this book may be reproduced in any form or by any electronic or mechanical means, including storage and retrieval systems, without express written permission, in writing, from the publisher.

Library of Congress Control Number – 2019903765

ISBN # 978-0-578-48732-8

Front cover design and layout by Brenna Woody

Printed and bound in the United States of America. For information, address Dogeared Press, P.O. Box 8306, Spring, TX 77380

Books may be purchased in bulk for promotional, educational, or business use. Please contact Dogeared Press and visit www.pushingforwardbook.com

Published by Dogeared Press
PO Box 8306
Spring, TX 77380

www.pushingforwardbook.com

Dedication

With love, respect and honor, I dedicate this work of literature to the lady who gave me life, guided me and allowed me to take this journey, Evangelist Minnie Lee Watkins. Without fear for herself, with full awareness of what could happen, and armed with the fortitude of foresight to know that living conditions for the Black race could not continue as they were, she gave her blessings to James Bevel to take me under his wings. With that, my journey as a Freedom Rider began.

I regret that her life span did not allow her to witness the election of the first African American President of the United States of America because she was an avid voter. And, I deeply regret that she is not here to read in print the journey that we took together in an effort to bring equality to our race and all mankind.

To my beloved wife, Chris Watkins, I thank you for all your love, guidance, encouragement, and patience with me throughout the years. It takes a great deal of compassion to love a person through all the tribulation that comes with being married to a Freedom Rider. I also want to thank my children and family for their continuous support along the way. A chance meeting…a shared love for history…a shared love for right and wrong…a shared love for all mankind….

To Andrea Ledwell, I give my sincere and heartfelt thanks for your friendship, sharing your family with mine, but most of all, I thank you for the love that has bonded our families.

What began as a casual conversation in Gallery 5 of the MS Civil Rights Museum birthed *Pushing Forward*. Thank you. The bond between our two families will forever be.

pushing *Forward*

The Story of Mississippi's Youngest Freedom Rider

Hezekiah Watkins
with Andrea Ledwell

Table of Contents

6	Introduction
11	Childhood
17	Who Are These Freedom Riders?
27	The First Push
37	The Buses Are A-Comin'
53	Beyond the Push
65	A Call to Action in Jackson
73	Freedom Summer and Beyond
82	Pursuing Equality
93	Passing the Torch
103	Where Do We Go From Here?
108	About the Author
110	Acknowledgments
111	Sources and Photo Credits

Introduction

I remember the first time I saw Mr. Watkins at the Mississippi Civil Rights Museum in Jackson. The previous couple of days was spent in Hattiesburg, Mississippi visiting family and working on a book I was writing at the time. While en route back to my home near Houston, Texas, I phoned my husband to tell him I decided to drive to Jackson to visit the Civil Rights Museum. Be it out of my way, this was something I'd been wanting to do since the museum's opening on December 9, 2017. I had just completed a short story about Mississippi Civil Rights featuring the Woolworth's Lunch Counter Sit-In of 1963 and I was eager to tour the museum.

After purchasing my ticket, I made my way through the main entrance. As I entered, a mural stood towering in front of me that read, "Mississippi Freedom Struggle." Making my way through the first exhibit, I could hear voices singing in the background, "Marching on to Freedom Land." As I turned around, I found myself in front of a huge placard that asked a simple question: "What are human rights?" The answer contained on the placard was as follows:

"A universal standard of treatment. All human beings are born free and equal in dignity and rights. They are endowed with reason and conscience and should act towards one another in a spirit of brotherhood." -United Nations Declaration of Human Rights, Article I, 1948

I lingered there a while, seeing pictures of slaves from long ago with shackles around them. Tears began to well up in my eyes as I thought to myself, "This really does say everything, doesn't it?"

As I made my way around the rest of the museum, each exhibit captivated and demanded my attention. I stopped periodically to chat with several attendants along the way. During a conversation with one of them, we began discussing the Freedom Riders and their brave efforts to challenge segregation with intrastate bus travel in the Jim Crow South. It was during this discussion that the museum attendant nonchalantly made the comment about how Mississippi's youngest Freedom Rider just so happened to work at the museum and was standing right over there; pointing his finger to a gentleman across the room. Although my exact words fail me now, I seem to remember it being somewhere along the lines of, "Get out of here!"

I looked over to see a gentleman neatly dressed in a red sweater vest smiling as he talked to a group of young teenagers. "I can introduce you to him if you'd like," commented the attendant. As I thanked the attendant and told him I'd love to meet him, I observed this mysterious gentleman from afar as he was interacting with the high schoolers across the room. At times he had a very serious expression on his face; he paused to point to his mugshot picture on the wall behind him, where he would tell a shortened version of how he was arrested. After a few moments, his expression changed, and a big smile would lit up across his face as he interacted with these students. During the entirety of this sequence of events, one thing was noticeable from the beginning: This younger generation of youth was completely focused, and they listened eagerly to every word he was saying. I then watched as all of them reached out to shake his hand and thanked him for talking with them.

When the group of teenagers departed, my new attendant friend introduced me to Mr. Watkins. He reached out and shook my hand, and then proceeded to tell me the story of how he became Mississippi's youngest Freedom Rider who was sent off to Parchman Penitentiary at the age of thirteen. The conversation that followed led to a series of events that would forever change my life; one of them is this story and the most important was that of a beautiful friendship. There was a gentleness in his voice that day which juxtaposed a serious tone as our dialogue went further. As Mr. Watkins stated to me that day, "You have your reason for being here at the museum today, and I have my reason for being here. For whatever reason, God allowed our paths to cross."

There was no way for me to fathom how many dots would be connected along this journey and throughout the course of this project. What you are about to read is the collaboration of two friends, who just so happen to be that of an older African-American gentleman, who lived through one of our country's most tumultuous eras, and a younger white woman, also from Mississippi who has experienced life through a very different prism. The irony of this hasn't escaped me, but rather I tend to view it as a milestone of how far we have come, and the way things should be. There was a time not too long ago, where this type of friendship and collaboration would've been unfathomable. Yet, here we are.

This book tells the story of Mississippi's youngest Freedom Rider in his own words. The information gathered in telling Mr. Watkins' story came from countless phone conversations and oral accounts in person with the two of us spending time together and visiting. Very little has been done to change the actual wording, phrasing, and description in Mr. Watkins' story. All the interviews that were conducted on my part, were transcribed and placed into a narrative format for reading. The reader should note that in the telling of this story, that the word "black" is used instead of African-American upon the insistence of Mr. Watkins during the first interview. It was important to have the story told exactly by Mr. Watkins, and every effort was made to keep it that way. The alternating chapters provide the reader with additional historical context, to better understand both the personal story and its importance in how it pieces together into a larger narrative during the Civil Rights Movement. The words and story belong to my good friend, Mr. Watkins. The lessons, however, are ours.

During one of the many conversations with Mr. Watkins, the two of us were talking together at the Civil Rights Museum in Jackson while he was on his break. At the time we were discussing the current racial climate in our country, bringing up certain examples here and there. At one point both of us found ourselves shaking our heads. I can remember looking to Mr. Watkins and asking the question, "Do you think we've learned anything from our past?" He responded by saying, "I'm not sure we have." There was silence and a moment of sadness. I then looked back at him and made the comment, "Where do we go from here?" It was at that point he looked over at me with a slight smile on his face and said, "You know, that's the same question that was always brought up at the end of all the meetings during The Movement; Where do we go from here?" To that we added, "We have to keep 'Pushing Forward.'

I'm still not sure what the answer is, but during these uncertain times, I think maybe it can begin with what the two of us have attempted to do with this book; One person, having the courage and wisdom to share his story and experiences so that others have the opportunity to learn and grow from them, and another person who's willing to listen, have those challenging conversations and take that knowledge and wisdom to pass it along to a younger generation.

I often think back to that first time I met my friend. Sometimes a chance encounter, a slight detour, or change of destination can lead us to the greatest of adventures in life. There's not a day that goes by I'm not thankful for meeting Mr. Watkins and the friendship we share. With all the wisdom, stories, and knowledge he's passed along to me over the duration of us getting to know one another, I can't help but think about how maybe we are all a part of something larger than ourselves. Maybe there's a single thread that is woven and interwoven across plane and time, and those threads might just happen to cross paths with others along our journey. Together they help form some beautiful, unseen tapestry that we have a chance to contribute to. The threads formed from all walks of life, ethnicities, cultures, and come together to create a spectacular mural of our lives. Captured within it, is our stories. The following is one that took a lifetime of bravery, persistence, and struggle to be told. It has been an honor to assist in its telling.

Andrea Ledwell

*"Without justice,
there can be no peace."*

-Dr. Martin Luther King Jr.

pushing FORWARD

CHAPTER ONE

CHILDHOOD

My name is Hezekiah Watkins. I was born in Milwaukee, Wisconsin. As a child I could have never imagined it would be the second of those two statements that would find its way back to haunt me at the age of thirteen.

My father, Willie Watkins, passed away when I was only a few months old. We were living in Milwaukee at the time. It wasn't too long before this my father made the decision to move our family to Wisconsin to join other relatives in search of a better life. This was not uncommon back then, as many of the black population of Mississippi was participating in a great exodus of the state known as the Great Migration. Our family being one of them.

It was upon my father's passing that my mother, Minnie Lee Watkins, decided to move my two older brothers and me back to Mississippi to a town called Pearson, adjacent to Rankin County. It was there my mother moved our family in with my grandparents. I can still remember how the house had no running water or indoor plumbing in those days. We lived there with my grandparents for years afterwards.

As the years passed, we moved two more times since the initial move into my grandparents' old house. The first house of our own had running water but no bathroom facilities. This was common place for the time. It was only when my mother got a job in Jackson that we were able to buy a home. The house I remember the most had both hot and cold running water, a real bathtub, and proved to be quite a unique experience for me. I felt we had moved from having nothing to gold. As the Jeffersons used to say, we were "movin' on up!" I still remember thinking that this was really the way to go. We had everything we needed, and life was good.

Before long, the time came for me to start school. The elementary school I attended was within walking distance from our house; about five or six blocks from where we lived. Of course, it was segregated. We lived behind Lamar Street, where the Greyhound Bus Station is located in Jackson. On the west side of Lamar is where the blacks lived. On the east side was where the whites lived. I can remember walking to school while the white kids rode the bus. We would see them each day on the way to school and they would yell at us from the bus windows. We would pick up rocks and throw them at the bus. This happened regularly.

However, as a child, I can recall playing with the white kids. Interactions such as these took place in the yard. Sometimes we would go into their backyard to shoot marbles or they would come into ours to play hopscotch or jump rope. However, we never went into their houses, and they didn't come into ours. There was an unwritten rule in Mississippi, which we all understood, that you didn't go any farther than the yard. If you wanted water or to use the bathroom, then you went home. In the days of my youth, even though blacks and whites might have lived close to one another, there was always something that separated you; a busy street, a railroad track, a vacant property; some kind of physical barrier that kept us away from one another. This was just the way of life for all of us as we knew it.

As I grew older, I often wondered why we were all going to separate schools. I didn't ask any adults and the kids never talked about the differences between the schools. I was never told the reason we attended different schools was because of color or segregation. The only explanation I received was, "They live on that side of the road, so they need to go to that school over there. You stay on this side of the road, so you go to school over here." That was the understanding that was given to not only me, but to all black kids. Blacks could not stay in white neighborhoods and vice-versa. I was very sheltered in terms of things I could and could not do in addition to the places I could and could not go. At night there was a street light outside of our house, and when that light came on, I knew I better have my butt at home. We were not roaming in the white neighborhood, or the black neighborhood for that matter. We weren't roaming period. There was no place we could be, other than at home, after dark.

As I continued to grow older, I accepted this kind of unspoken rule that blacks and whites were supposed to be separate, without ever truly understanding why. After time went by, it slowly became a way of life. You accepted this unspoken rule, but at the same time, you were never told the reason why all of this is going on. Deep down you knew there was something left untold. Your parents didn't tell you back then, and you didn't dare ask them why certain things were as they were. You made the adjustment whenever it was necessary, and that was that. Each person just dealt with this in their own way; accepting it as a way of life. And that's exactly what it was; an all-encompassing way of life. Just like when we had Bible study every Wednesday, I never questioned it. I just accepted it was how things were. In return, that's how I have dealt with segregation all my life. It was an unwritten rule, but you understood that rule, without the rule ever really being told to you, and you didn't dare do anything to break that rule.

My daily schedule consisted of a routine and certain activities a young child my age would often do. Once we got out of the bed each morning, we had to make up our beds, and we were not allowed to get back in them until it was time to go to sleep for the night. When school was out for the day, you didn't just lie around being unproductive. Instead, you did something to help bring a dollar to the table. There was no down time. I can remember going into the briar patch and picking berries. My mother would make cobblers with them. We also had a lot of plum trees and I used to sell them downtown. My friends and I would often go from one business to another, asking if anyone wanted to buy plums. Some businesses would buy from us and some wouldn't. If a particular business didn't, we would move on to the next. Boy, those were the days!

Aside from school, picking berries and selling plums, there weren't a lot of things I was allowed to do. This applied to the other kids in our neighborhood as well. My mother, for one, was a religious fanatic. I believed in God but Mom took it to another level. While the other kids could play typical childhood games of the time, we were not allowed to shoot marbles, play cards, etc. at least when my mother was around. The only game we were allowed to play was cowboys. Sometimes we would play ball, but never on Sundays. Here lied a dilemma. After church was over, that was the time everybody in the neighborhood wanted to play. My brothers and I were told to change out of our "good Sunday clothes" and put on our other clothes, as to not ruin them, and we would do just that. However, we then found ourselves with nothing to do because all the other kids were playing ball or some other type of sports. My mother believed you weren't supposed to do any of those things on Sunday. That was God's day, and we couldn't participate. Her word was the gospel truth, and we didn't dare question it, although we secretly fumed about it.

Being the youngest of three boys, my mother was strict with us, and I suppose she had to be. She raised us no different than any other child in the south. We were raised to respect our elders, or any elders for that matter, regardless of color. We were taught to say, "Yes Sir and No Ma'am." Those are qualities I still have in me to this day; not because of color, but because of age. It was just the way we were taught. We were also taught The Golden Rule: to treat your fellow man the way you want him to treat you.

One of the most important lessons my mother taught me was to never tell a lie. I remember getting so many whoopin's for small, little lies. As a child I was always told that a small lie would lead to a larger lie, and a larger lie would land you in jail. That was always my Momma's saying. "It's gonna land you in jail or hell." I didn't understand either jail or hell in terms of where it's gonna land me, but when Momma said it, I believed it.

"Hallelujah I'm a travelin'
Hallelujah ain't it fine.
Hallelujah I'm a travelin'
Down Freedom's main line!"

Sung by Freedom Riders

pushing FORWARD

CHAPTER TWO

Who Are These Freedom Riders?

In July of 1944, a black woman named of Irene Morgan from Baltimore, Maryland was traveling by bus to visit her mother in Gloucester County, Virginia. After her visit, she boarded a Greyhound bus and sat next to another black woman holding an infant. During this time, there were no "rules" designating where blacks or whites were to sit while traveling on a bus, but it was an unspoken rule that blacks could not sit next to or across from a white passenger.

Upon a stop in Middlesex County, Virginia, a white couple boarded, and the driver ordered both Morgan and her seatmate to give up their seats to them. As the seatmate surrendered her seat to move to the back of the bus, Morgan refused. The bus driver then got off the bus to find a sheriff to demand that Morgan move to the back, but again she refused to give up her seat. A warrant was then issued to Morgan to which she tore up in front of the sheriff and threw out the bus window. An altercation then resulted between the two which led to Morgan's arrest for violation of Virginia's Jim Crow transit law.

The term "Jim Crow" dates back to the 1800's to an old song which was preformed in blackface to make a satire out of slaves. The word "Jim" was used to describe a way of loosening something "Jimmy" it and was often used by means of a crowbar (crows, also being black in color). The term as we now know it is a systematic way of providing racial oppressions towards blacks by whites.

With Maryland not enforcing Virginia's Jim Crow law and it not applying to Morgan, her case was then taken to the Virginia Supreme Court, which found her in violation of the law, but ultimately led to victory in the U.S. Supreme Court.

Irene Morgan vs. Commonwealth of Virginia in 1946 ruled that segregation on interstate travel violated the Interstate Commerce Clause of the U.S. Constitution. It was a short-lived victory in which the Jim Crow South refused to abide. No immediate changes took place after the ruling in terms of bus regulations or with the likelihood of blacks changing their seating positions from the back of the bus to the front. The court case failed to designate when and how the integration of bus travel should take place thus stating when black passengers traveled through states with segregation laws, they should be seated in the back with white passengers towards the front. It wasn't long before other bus companies followed Greyhound's "Seating of Passengers in Coaches" memo.

Civil Rights Activist, Rosa Parks, also refused to give up her seat one December day in 1955 when be bus driver moved the colored sign to redesignate the colored section. Three other black passengers agreed to move, but Rosa refused, stating she was tired (not physically, but rather tired of complying and giving into Jim Crow). She was then arrested in violation of Chapter six, Section eleven of the Montgomery City Code and was taken to jail. The Montgomery Bus Boycott was then organized by the local chapter of the NAACP which lasted for three-hundred and eighty-one days. The boycott led to the burning of black churches and Dr. Martin Luther King Jr.'s house being bombed in an attempt to end the boycott. The boycott came to an official end on December 20, 1956 and was known as the biggest and most successful mass movements against Jim Crow yet.

December 5, 1960 Boynton vs. Virginia ruled that segregation was not only illegal on buses, trains or airplanes but also in terminals because it violated the Interstate Commerce Act. It was also ruled illegal to have segregated restrooms, water fountains or lunch counters. This was an important ruling which allowed the Federal Government to now regulate and forbid discrimination in the interstate commerce industry.

Meanwhile, James Farmer Jr., born in Marshall, Texas and the youngest debater of the famous Wiley College debate team under Professor Melvin Tolson, was taking note of the current ruling and of the Jim Crow South's refusal to abide. Farmer's time at Wiley College, and famous winning debate at the University of Southern California, led him to follow in the footsteps of Mohandas Gandhi; implementing a method of nonviolent civil disobedience to challenge segregation laws. Upon his graduation from Wiley College, his father, James Farmer Sr., asked of his son just one question, "What are you going to do with your education?" James Farmer Jr. answered with a simple, yet profound response: "Destroy Segregation."

It was the ruling of the Boynton vs. Virginia case that caught James Farmer Jr.'s attention. Having led the first nonviolent sit-in to desegregate a lunch counter in Chicago, Farmer had his eye on the ruling and sought to challenge the Jim Crow South's noncompliance of it.

In 1961, Farmer was appointed national director of Congress of Racial Equality, or C.O.R.E., an African-American Civil Rights organization in which Farmer was a founding member in 1942. C.O.R.E.'s non-violent methods had been increasingly effective in desegregating schools, housing and employment in the North, and quickly spread across the country as local chapters trained members in non-violent techniques.

An idea came forth to challenge the noncompliance of the Morgan vs. Virginia ruling by utilizing the intrastate buses with both the Trailways and Greyhound lines by sending them into parts of the south still abiding by the Jim Crow travel laws. The team would consist of black and white participants who would refuse to accept the Jim Crow laws of segregation, not only on the buses, but also on the bus terminals, restaurants, waiting rooms, and restrooms. This courageous group of passengers who would dare take on the challenges of tackling segregation head-on and demand freedom for all. They would become known as the Freedom Riders.

A test ride had actually taken place fourteen years earlier, in 1947, called the Journey of Reconciliation which served to test the waters of challenging segregation. The Freedom Ride of 1961 would differ from the former in three distinct ways: The first and most significant point of distinction was the Freedom Rides ability to penetrate the deep south, rather than just the upper south. The second distinction would involve participants not only integrating the bus seating but also involved the facilities of bus travel. Finally, the riders would be committed to adopting a policy of remaining in jail if arrested and insisting on no bail.

All participants in the Freedom Ride were required to apply through C.O.R.E and promised to employ only non-violent means, even if they were attacked. These methods were extremely effective, designed to expose the violence of the Jim Crow South against anyone daring to stand in its way. Aspiring Freedom Riders were to understand and uphold the following before being considered for the rides.

"I wish to apply for acceptance as a participant in C.O.R.E's Freedom Ride 1961, to travel via bus from Washington D.C. to New Orleans, LA to test and challenge segregated facilities en route. I understand that I shall be participating in a non-violent protest against racial discrimination, that arrest or personal injury to me might result, and that, by signing this application, I waive all rights to damages against C.O.R.E."

So who were these people so committed to challenging segregation in the south that they would willingly risk personal injury, attacks and possible death for freedom and equality for all? The original Freedom Riders trained by C.O.R.E. were as follows:

Julia Aaron, Mr. and Mrs. Walter Bergman, Albert Bigelow, Edward Blankenheim, Doris Castle, B.Elton Cox, Dave Dennis, James Farmer, Herman Harris, Genevieve Hughes, Jean Lewis, Jimmie McDonald, Ivor Moore, Mae Frances Moultrie, Jim Peck, Joseph Perkins, Charles Person, Isaac Reynolds, Jerome Smith, Henry Thomas and Jean Thompson.

It was a beautiful day in Washington D.C. on May 4th, 1961 as thirteen Freedom Riders loaded the buses, and a spirit of anticipation and happiness hung in the air. There was a sense purpose, and liberation; dedication to the movement and a good feeling that encompassed each participant. Sure, there was an anticipation of not being served at restaurants or possible arrests for purposely challenging the segregated rules of the Jim Crow South; however, nothing beyond those experiences would happen. If an altercation were to occur, then CORE's training of nonviolent techniques would be utilized and employed. Each Freedom Rider knew of the challenges that awaited them, yet their dedication to getting the movement into the deep south in hopes of starting a national movement was behind each person willing to face such obstacles.

It was decided the group would be split; seven blacks and six whites, utilizing both the Trailways and Greyhound Buses on regularly scheduled routes. The first few days proved to be relatively uneventful for the Freedom Riders and filled them with a false sense of confidence that maybe the task of challenging segregation laws wouldn't be quite as hard as had been expected. In fact, this was turning out to be a piece of cake.

The first real action the Riders experienced took place in Charlotte, North Carolina on May 8th. While stopped at the bus station, Joseph Perkins was arrested for trespassing charges for attempting to have his shoes shined at a whites-only shoeshine chair. Two days later, Perkins was found to be innocent due to Boynton vs. Virginia and was released. The group now made their way into Rock Hill, South Carolina.

While at a Greyhound Bus Terminal, John Lewis, Al Bigelow and Genevieve Hughes entered a whites only waiting room. An altercation occurred which resulted with injuries sustained by the three riders. The attack was broken up by the police, and the Freedom Riders would now make their way into Atlanta where a reception would await them by Dr. Martin Luther King Jr.

Leaving South Carolina for Atlanta filled the Freedom Riders with a sense of excitement. Each of them was eager to meet Dr. King and ultimately hoped to have him join the Freedom Rides with them to further the cause of the movement. Although a few black members of the press had originally joined the group on its departure from Washington D.C., there was no national recognition in the Freedom Rides. By having Dr. King to ride on the buses with them, this would certainly bring attention to CORE and the movement, which would help with funding their cause.

Following the reception, Dr. King visited with the Freedom Riders and discussed their requests to have him join the group. They became disappointed when Dr. King refused to participate. His explanation to the Riders was he felt the Freedom Rides might do more harm in the movement than good and furthermore, he had recently received a warning from his sources in Alabama that the Klan was preparing something for the Riders once they made their way across the state line. Later in the evening, more bad news awaited the Riders as word was sent to James Farmer that his father had passed away. This meant that Farmer, their leader, would now be leaving the group just when they were about to set off for the most dangerous leg of their trip. Jim Peck now placed himself in the role as leader and for the first time, a tense and uncertain mood stirred in the Riders.

It was a bright and beautiful Mother's Day morning in Atlanta. Two buses departed for Birmingham, Alabama; one Trailways and one Greyhound. The group had been split once again with the two buses having left Atlanta one hour apart. Even with Dr. King's warning of the Klan, there wasn't a sense of fear present. The group of Freedom Riders aboard the Greyhound Bus left first and made their way to Birmingham. When they arrived in the city of Anniston, the Klan would be waiting for them. As the Greyhound pulled into the station, an angry mob of close to two-hundred people gathered around the bus station. They shouted things like "Let's kill these niggers," and "nigger-lovers." Within minutes the mob was breaking out windows in the bus and puncturing its tires. The attack lasted nearly fifteen minutes, and the bus was able to leave the station once the drivers were switched. Once out of the station, a car in front of the bus was busy swerving in the road to keep the Greyhound from getting by. Around this time, the air was completely out of the tires and the bus was pulled over on the side of the road. Once the driver saw the flat tires, he abandoned the bus and all its passengers.

Within minutes, the mob was back shouting, "Let's burn them niggers!" A man with a crowbar swung and broke out one of the back windows and then lifted his arm back to launch a firebomb inside the broken window. It was at this time the Riders started to fear the situation they now found themselves in and panicked. Just then, the fuel tank of the bus exploded, letting off thick billows of black smoke inside. The crowd of passengers inside ran and managed to push the doors of the bus open to escape. Once outside, the Freedom Riders were struggling to breathe and gasping for air. Hank Thomas was beaten over the head with a baseball bat after a man asked him if he was alright. After managing to crawl away, another five men started coming for him. Just then, the highway patrolman fired his gun into the air and said, "Okay. You've had your fun. Let's move back."

Meanwhile, the Trailways bus with the second group of Freedom Riders was making its way into Birmingham, unaware of the horror the first group encountered in Anniston. Birmingham was a police state, with Bull Connor at its center as the Commissioner of Public Safety. Little did the second group of Freedom Riders know that lurking in the shadows of Birmingham was a shady deal struck by Bull Connor with the Klan, stating that he would give them roughly fifteen minutes to do whatever they wanted to these outside agitators, who were attempting to disrupt their so-called Southern way of life. Not a soul would be arrested for it. As so, a fiery cross would stand as a call to signal Klansmen from all over the south to Birmingham.

When the bus arrived, the Freedom Riders were met by an angry mob numbering well into the thousands. Charles Person and James Peck were assigned to test the facilities and as they exited the bus, they found the station lined with men toting anything from bats and clubs to guns and metal pipes. Each had their eyes on these outside agitators and were ready to bloody and kill them. Within moments, the mob attacked and a violent brawl ensued. James Peck was knocked down immediately and bloodied. A violent rage for nearly ten minutes would ensue, the likes of which no one had ever seen or captured in photographs. As if almost on cue, the Birmingham police came filing in from up the street only after the mob fled. This horrific attack left the Freedom Riders with nine brutally injured. James Peck released a statement after leaving the hospital that "we must not surrender to violence" and insisted the Freedom Rides continue. A new challenge now faced the group when trying to leave the bus station. With a mob still present, along with the police, no drivers dared to operate the bus, leaving the Freedom Riders stranded. John Seigenthaler, Assistant to the U.S. Attorney General, was in communication with Bobby Kennedy and it was decided the federal government would need to step in to safely get them out of Birmingham. The Riders left for New Orleans by means of a plane.

With what seemed to be a horrible situation somewhat settled, it would only be a short time before Bobby Kennedy would be asking the question, "Who the hell is Diane Nash?" regarding another wave of Freedom Riders making their way to Birmingham, only this time from Nashville. It seemed like James Peck's call to continue was heard. This time, however, SNCC- The Student Nonviolent Coordinating Committee, led by Nash, would be sending in Freedom Riders. Ten students from SNCC were selected to ride into Birmingham on a Greyhound Bus to pick up where the original Freedom Riders left off. Upon arrival, Bull Connor immediately had them arrested. The next day, the group was released from jail and escorted to the Alabama/Tennessee state line and left there. The group would seek shelter in a local's house. Another group of fresh Freedom Riders from Nashville made their way into Birmingham but now found themselves stuck at the station with no drivers willing to take the risk. While at the bus station, the Riders now found themselves face to face with the Klan, dressed in sheets taunting them. At the same time, talks were attempted between Bobby Kennedy and Governor John Patterson of Alabama to address the safety and protection of the Freedom Riders. Police protection would come in the form of state troopers escorting the Riders to Montgomery, where upon reaching the city, everything turned eerily calm.

Montgomery would prove to be the turning point, as matters escalated to unprecedented violence within no time. Out of nowhere, a white mob numbering close to three hundred attacked the students. There were no police to be found. Beatings, attacks, and rioting continued. John Seigenthaler was hit over the head with a pipe and left unconscious while trying to intervene. Tear gas was released by the police to break up the mob, but not without leaving twenty people hurt and bloodied. It was apparent to the Kennedy administration that Gov. Patterson was unwilling to ensure the safety of the Freedom Riders in Alabama and federal troops were subsequently sent in.

The following evening, it was determined The Movement would now back the efforts of the Freedom Riders, and a meeting would be held to support them at Reverend Abernathy's church in Montgomery. Some fifteen hundred people would be in attendance that night including the Freedom Riders, Dr. King, Fred Shuttlesworth, and James Farmer. However, the angry white mob wasn't done yet. They were gathering outside of the church, and the taunting started to escalate from throwing rocks at the church windows to setting fire around its perimeter. The marshals released tear gas into the rioters but ended up failing due to a strong wind, turning the tear gas on themselves. With people trapped inside and the violence quickly escalating, Dr. King placed a call to Bobby Kennedy urging him to have the federal government step in and do something. Gov. Patterson was unwilling to take responsibility to put a stop to the rioting, leaving Bobby Kennedy no choice but to declare the city to be under Marshall Law. Eight hundred national guard troops were called in to put an end to the rioting.

For the first time, what took place in Montgomery helped shed light on the extreme violence and unrelenting ways of the South to yield to the federal ruling of desegregation. The Civil Rights Movement now had the attention of the Kennedy Administration, and the next stop would be Jackson, Mississippi.

> *"I think a hero is an ordinary individual who finds strength to persevere and endure in spite of overwhelming obstacles."*
>
> Christopher Reeves, Superman

pushing *FORWARD*

CHAPTER THREE

The First Push

At first, I really didn't understand who these Freedom Riders were. The topic was kept very hushed and no one talked about it. Of course, this occurred about six years after the death of Emmett Till. We weren't told anything about him either. Everything was a secret to us during that time. Not even our parents, pastors, principals or teachers dared speak about it. Most of the black community got much of our information from Jet Magazine. As kids in the neighborhood began to talk, word got around the cause of Emmett Till's death was a result of him touching a white woman's butt. None of this made sense to me. Then I became curious. In the mind of a young child, I began to wonder what was so special about a woman's butt, or in particular, a white woman's butt. I was just naïve. It was at that point when my mother began to tell me about white folks and black folks. It wasn't until that particular moment that I began to be told anything related to blacks and whites, and even then it was very little.

From that moment, I was told that when you see white folks, especially if they are female, that you look downward to the ground. You don't look up and whatever you do, under no circumstances do you look them in the eyes. If a white person was walking towards you down the sidewalk, then you should step aside into the street in order to let them pass, and you always replied with a "Yes

Sir" or "Yes Ma'am." These were things that were told to me during this time. It was understood by all blacks that this was how things were. Growing up as a child in the south, you didn't dare ask anyone to explain these things to you. If you happened to end up asking someone other than your parents why these things were the way they were, the only response you would receive would be, "You don't want to end up like Emmett Till, do you?" That ended any discussion before one ever began.

It was around the end of my eighth-grade year of school at Rowan that I started to hear of these Freedom Riders. During this time they were in Alabama along their route, challenging segregation with buses and terminals in the south. We were able to see all the beatings taking place on TV, and it just seemed unreal to me. A few weeks before school ended, I remember the principal had a meeting in the auditorium telling all the students these so-called Freedom Riders were making their way into Jackson and to not get involved. We were told that being involved in any way with this group of people could bring great harm to you and your parents. We were then told about how houses had been burned, lynchings had taken place, and all kinds of other bad things that were happening. This was even discussed at church. The preacher spoke about it from the pulpit, and my mother discussed the topic on the way home from church. As I mentioned before, if my mother told me something, I didn't dare go against it. It was enough by her telling me not to get involved, so I had no plans to.

You can imagine what curiosity and confusion this stirred up in the mind of a young, thirteen-year-old boy. I had been watching all these activities taking place on TV, and then I'm heard about them at school. All the while, I'm not fully understanding what was really happening. I remember hearing some people say at the time how the Freedom Riders were fighting for rights and equality. I know this seemed a little far-fetched, but I thought, "Rights? The right to do what? Look at butts?" In my mind, I related what little I knew back to the misinformation I heard about Emmett Till.

While watching the news, it was this type of reasoning that was still circling my mind. I began to wonder why police officers were beating these black guys all because of looking at somebody's butt, or for looking some white woman in the eyes. I started looking for white girls on TV to understand (I was allowed to look at them on TV, I suppose) but I never saw any of them doing these things, so I started to become very confused.

A few weeks later, things were really starting to get heated in Jackson. I believe the first Freedom Rider was arrested around June. There were a lot of media outlets covering the Freedom Riders, although I don't recall any of them being beaten. We heard a group of them was going to be in Jackson at the Greyhound Bus Station. A friend of mine by the name of Troy, suggested that we should go over there to have a better look just to be nosy. We just knew these individuals had to be supernatural humans based on what we witnessed on TV that took place in Alabama. The images we watched on the news showed how they were being beaten, kicked, sprayed with water hoses, bitten by dogs... all kinds of harmful and inhumane treatment that was being handed down to them, yet they couldn't be stopped. Every time they got knocked down or beaten, they kept coming back for more. I just knew there had to be some kind of special clothing they were wearing for protection. We were thinking there must've been something on them in terms of a shield or guard that was preventing them from being hurt; like something a superhero would wear for protection. No regular human being could withstand that type of brutal punishment. For a 13 year-old boy, there could be no other explanation than the Freedom Riders must be superheroes. We needed a closer look and it was decided. After we finished attending the mass meeting, we would go by the Greyhound Bus Station to check out the Freedom Riders.

When Troy and I got down to the bus station, there were crowds of people. We didn't have a good view from where we were standing, and we couldn't see any of the Freedom Riders up close to inspect their clothing. It was at this point that Troy suggested we should just run across the street to get a better view of what was happening. The idea was to quickly run past the entrance to the door of the Greyhound Bus Station and keep going. We would then circle back around and do it all over again. This way, we could get a good view of the Freedom Riders and really see what their protective clothing looked like up close. We had no intentions of getting in the middle of things, but the idea to get a closer look was one we couldn't pass up.

We mustered up the courage and decided to go for it! It was as we were passing by the entrance of the door to the Greyhound Bus Station, that Troy decided it would be a funny joke to push me inside. And that's exactly what he did. Before I realized it, I was mixed up in the crowd of Freedom Riders inside the station. Sheer panic rushed over me. I tried to break free and run out, but just as I did an officer blocked my path and prevented me from leaving. When my friend saw that a police officer now had me, he took off running and didn't look back.

Years later, Troy would corroborate the events of that day with one big exception: He would claim that he tried to prevent me from entering the building and was instead trying to pull me back outside. I suppose it's up to you as to which version you believe, but I'm telling you right now that I was pushed. After all the warnings I heard from everyone in the community and the potential harm of getting involved with the Freedom Riders, I wasn't looking for trouble. It was enough for my mother to tell me to stay away. Now, here I was right in the middle of the trouble I had been warned constantly to avoid.

With Troy nowhere in sight, and now in the hands of the police, I found myself in a huge dilemma. I was right in the middle of the Freedom Riders. The curiosity of the superhuman clothing was now an afterthought. The officer told me to take a seat, so I did. About fifteen to twenty minutes later, the same officer came back and asked me two questions:

"What is your name and place of birth?"

I told him my name was Hezekiah Watkins, and my place of birth was Milwaukee, Wisconsin." He then replied, "Oh. Okay." I didn't know what he meant by his reply but was later told that he was thinking that I was one of the Freedom Riders that came in from another state, an outside agitator. These Freedom Riders were all young students, so I suppose I can see where there might be some confusion. He then shouted, "We've got another one over here!"

I was detained for maybe an hour, and then put into the back of a paddy wagon and taken straight to the state prison in Mississippi, named Parchman. I was alone, with no other Freedom Rider with me in the back of the paddy wagon. I had no idea what was going on or where they were taking me. I was also incredibly scared. The ride to Parchman took a long time. In fact, I fell asleep in the back along the way. I estimated the time we arrived at Parchman being around five or six hours after we left the Greyhound Bus Station in Jackson.

Parchman Penitentiary was opened in 1880 and served as a means of Jim Crow Justice, which meant unfairly convicting blacks and using them as unpaid farm laborers for the state. This was how slavery survived the Civil War in Mississippi. I, being thirteen at the time, knew none of this. I was very sheltered in terms of these things. It was only just recently that my mother explained to me a little bit about the interactions between whites and blacks as a way of life in the south. I wondered if Troy was back home telling my mom about what had happened to me, and if she would be worried. I had no idea what to expect next or what would happen to me. I was in the hands of the police, and they were now in charge of me.

After my arrival to Parchman, an officer woke me up in the back of the paddy wagon and led me to a building where I had to turn in all of my belongings. I didn't have anything on me other than the clothes I was wearing. After that, they walked me down the hall and led me on to a cell. I don't remember much about that first night other than being scared and not knowing what was going on.

The next morning, I was awakened by two inmates who were sharing the cell with me. As we began to talk, they started telling me all kinds of things about the crimes I probably committed which would've landed me there at Parchman. You can imagine how a sheltered, 13 year-old boy could feel at hearing some of the things being discussed by these inmates. I was just a school boy, but now I found myself receiving a whole new kind of education. Confused and trying to make sense as to what was taking place, I told them I hadn't committed any crime and the only thing I did was to be pushed into the Greyhound Bus Station. One of them said, "Ah… you did more than that," insisting this couldn't be the whole story. I remember telling them I hadn't done anything other than what I just described.

Eventually, one of the guys told me, "Well, I know what happened." Still confused and eager to find out what he knew, I listened carefully so he could actually inform me of why I ended up being sent here.

"You must've raped a white woman," the inmate replied.

"No!" I shouted, being scared out of my shoes. I remember tears coming to my eyes at that point as I said, "I haven't raped anybody," to which the inmate said, "Well you must've done something as bad for you to be here on Death Row."

"Death Row." I had never heard those two words before in my life. I didn't know the meaning of the term "Death Row." Just earlier in the day I was wanting to get a closer look at the superhuman-Freedom Rider's protective clothing and now here I was... the same 13 year-old boy hearing the phrase, "Death Row." I remember asking one of the inmates what Death Row was and he told me, "That's where they fry your ass." At this time, I was still trying to process all this information and not really knowing what these two inmates were talking about, feeling extremely baffled and now trembling from fright.

The next day, the inmates and I got a little more comfortable talking with each other, but they kept telling me, "Your ass is gonna be fried!" At one point, still trying to make sense of things, I said, "Please explain to me what it means when they "fry your ass?"

One of the inmates laughed at this and pointed, "They gonna take you right around the corner there, and once you get around that corner, they gonna hook you up to the gas chamber. Once that happens, you get gone."

I said, "Gone?"

"Yeah. They gonna kill you!"

It was at this point I began to worry about people at Parchman killing me, and I began to fear for my life. It had never entered my mind until that moment. All these things became a huge problem and introduced to me a new world I had never encountered before. I received an education that day, only the kind of education someone never imagines receiving, much less that of a naive 13year-old boy.

As if this weren't concern enough to give me nightmares, the following day the inmates began to give little gestures and make statements about me being their "friend." Before long, they began to argue about whose friend I was going to be, so I told them, "I want to be friends with both of you."

One inmate said, "No. You just gonna be my friend.

I had no idea just what type of friendship they were talking about. In my mind, the only friendship I knew was the type I had back in my neighborhood with people my own age. I couldn't understand why they weren't satisfied with us all being friends.

Then the other inmate said, "Nah… You gonna be my bitch." Now I'd heard the term "bitch" before, but it was always done in a slang-type of manner. It really did not register with me what he meant by using the term in that way.

At one point I recall one of them pulling me to him and feeling on me. The other inmate got mad when he saw this happening. A verbal altercation took place between the two of them. At this point, I was still in the dark as to what was going on, and I'm thinking to myself, "Why is this man feeling on me? I'm a boy. He's a boy. Why is he doing this?"

Nothing other than this one incident happened to me during my time at Parchman with these two inmates. These guys were hardened criminals who had committed violent acts and were awaiting their time on Death Row. Still, I wish I would've thought to get their names and information, so I could've reached out to their relatives at some point down the road. However, at the age of 13, all that was on my mind during my time at Parchman was trying to stay alive.

Later that day, the guard called my name and told me to get my belongings. Since I didn't have any belongings on me when I was arrested, they opened the cell and walked me out. As I was being escorted outside, I was once again placed inside of a paddy wagon, only this time they drove me back to Jackson. I had no idea where I was going.

"Governor Ross Barnett ordered your release," said an officer once we started driving. Relief instantly found me inside of that paddy wagon as I made the long journey back to Jackson.

During my time at Parchman, Troy did not tell my mother, or his mother, what had happened. He was afraid that by telling someone what took place, that he would've received what was called a "beatdown." Remember, during this time we were all told by everyone in our community to stay away from these Freedom Riders and to not get mixed up with them, or great harm would come to us and our families. Here I was right in the middle of it all. Troy was out during my time at Parchman, leading the search party with everyone back home looking for me. To this day I don't think he ever told his mother what really happened.

After a day went by and I didn't show up at home, my mother immediately knew that something had to be terribly wrong. She then decided to go out looking for me in the neighborhood, asking people in the community if they'd seen me and started calling all the law agencies within a certain number of miles.

During this time, my mother worked as the head chef at Primos, which was a five-star restaurant in Jackson. When she couldn't find me, she went to the owner of the restaurant, who was a white man, and he tried to help locate me. When he ended up with no luck, my mother really began to panic. She was thinking to herself, "Could what happened to Emmett Till have happened to my son?" In fact, I'm sure that's what she was thinking. Another Emmett Till. After all, blacks were coming up missing around this time. Most of them, their bodies were never recovered.

After a few days of frantic searching, my mother received a phone call from the Jackson Police Department telling her to come pick up her son from the station. Nothing was told to her about the state of my condition, so my mother actually thought she was going to identify my body.

My mother arrived at the police department with the minister who escorted her inside. It was then she first saw me, and she then started hugging on me like you wouldn't believe. She began asking questions such as, "Everything okay, baby? Did they beat you? You look okay, is anything hurting you?" You know, all the things a mother would say to her child to ensure he or she was alright.

I kept telling my mother, "I'm fine. Everything's okay. I'm okay." Before I was released back into my mother's custody, she was instructed to sign a release form stating that I would not have any further actions with the Freedom Riders or else I would not be let go. She signed the papers, handed them back to the police officer, and held me close to her as we made our way back home. I wasn't allowed to talk about my ordeal at Parchman, my arrest, or anything that took place.

Once we got home, my moment of being okay was short-lived as my mother told me to get my own switches from the Pisselm Tree. She then plaited the long branches together. I was then told to get inside the house and "drop 'em." I knew exactly what she meant by that too. It meant, take off all your clothes, even your unders. I did just that and my mom proceeded to beat me severely for getting involved with those Freedom Riders I had specifically been told to stay away from, causing her to fear her son might be dead.

My stay at Parchman Penitentiary lasted a total of five days; however, it felt as if it were for five months. After my time spent there, I was forever changed.

"Buses are a comin' Oh Yes!
Buses are a comin' Oh Yes!
Buses are a comin' Buses are a comin'
Buses are a comin' Oh Yes!"

Song created by Freedom Riders to taunt prison guards

pushing FORWARD

CHAPTER FOUR

The Buses Are A-Comin'

In 1955, a young fourteen-year-old boy from Chicago named Emmett Till decided to make a summer trip in August to visit relatives near the small town of Money, Mississippi. Emmett's mother, Mamie, was born in Webb, Mississippi but moved with her family to Argo, Illinois as part of the Great Migration of black families to escape the danger and violence of the south. The degree of this movement that Mamie and her family participated in was to such an extent that Argo earned the nickname of being called "Little Mississippi."

Mamie and Emmett lived on the south side of Chicago and enjoyed a life together surrounded by family, in which Mamie raised Emmett almost entirely on her own after Louis Till, Emmett's father, had died.

Emmett was a delightful son, who helped his mother willingly with chores around the house and who loved to laugh. Like most boys his age, Emmett also loved baseball. He rooted for the Brooklyn Dodgers, seeing how they were able to break the color barrier by bringing on Jackie Robinson in 1947, with his hero being Don Newcombe who also pitched for the Dodgers. Emmett and his mother were also very close. It was with a persistent urging from Emmett, and a great deal of reluctance, that Mamie agreed to allow her son to visit with family back in Mississippi. Before boarding the train, Mamie instructed Emmett on the customs of being in Mississippi; the same instructions given to all black children in the south, "Say yes ma'am and no sir, do not start a conversation with a white person, step aside if a white man or woman is walking towards you, and look downward- never in their eyes." It was with this understanding that Emmett said goodbye to this mother and left to meet Uncle Moses in Mississippi.

On the evening of August 24th, 1955, Rev. Moses Wright decided to let Emmett, his three sons, and Wheeler Parker borrow his Ford pickup after spending the day picking cotton. The boys drove to the Bryant's Grocery Store in Money, a place known to locals in the black community for being able to congregate on the porch and playing a game of checkers. Emmett wasn't too far behind as Wheeler Parker went in first to purchase some candy. Emmett was in the store with owner Carolyn Bryant for only a few minutes, but it was during that time his fate had been sealed.

There is much speculation as to what occurred during that brief time in the store. As Carolyn Bryant would go on to state in a private conversation with her attorney, she "waited on him and when I went to take his money, he grabbed my hand and said how about a date, and I walked away from him, and he said, What's the matter baby, can't you take it? He went out the door and said goodbye and I went to the car and got the pistol. When I came back, he whistled at me." Some reports account for Carolyn Bryant and her husband Roy, becoming offended when Emmett waved goodbye at her. Others state it was his failure to say, "Yes Ma'am" when talking to Mrs. Bryant. Others discuss physical assault. What is known is that at the age of six, a young Emmett was stricken with Polio and survived, but not after being left with life-long disabilities which included permanent limb damage and a noticeable stutter. Could that have possibly been the wolf-whistle as Mrs. Bryant went to retrieve the pistol from her car?

When Roy Bryant found out about the incident, he and his half-brother, J.W. Milam, went to Rev. Wright's house to find Emmett and abduct him. Once in their possession, Emmett was taken to a shed in Drew, MS where they proceeded to pistol whip the young boy, beating him ruthlessly until he was knocked unconscious, then shooting him above his right ear. He was then tied up with several feet of barbed wire, along with a fan weighing about 150 pounds, and then dumped into the

Tallahatchie River. When the body was discovered three days later by a local on the river checking his fishing lines, the authorities were contacted and the body of young Emmett Till was exhumed. His face was badly mutilated and looked as if someone had taken an ax to it. His right eye was protruding from its socket, and there was a bullet wound above his right ear.

Once his mother was notified of her son's brutal death, a courageous Mamie decided to allow for an open casket, as to let the world see what had happened to her son in Mississippi. The world watched the events unfold. There would be a trial, although no black jurors would be selected. In the end, Roy Bryant and his half-brother, J.W. Milam, would walk away being found not guilty by an all-white jury of the murder they had committed. Emmett Till was only fourteen. His death sparked a renewed commitment to the Civil Rights Movement that fired up the nation in an unrelenting Jim Crow South. It was with the death of Emmett Till in mind that Hezekiah's mother, Minnie, feared her young son's disappearance (close in age to Emmett Till) would result in a similar outcome. It was also the territory of white supremacy fearing no consequences in committing such brutal atrocities to blacks, and those who identified with them, that the Freedom Riders now made their way into Mississippi.

Escorted by law enforcement and the national guard, The Freedom Riders crossed the state line out of Alabama and were greeted by a sign that read, "Welcome to Mississippi, the Magnolia State." After the experiences in Alabama, no one knew what to expect. It felt as if they had entered a foreign land. Everyone knew about the horrific death of Emmett Till, and after the violence experienced in Alabama, one could only fathom that Mississippi would hold worse things in store. Just a little way up the road the next sign read, "Prepare to meet thy God," and fear now set in for the Freedom Riders.

The night before in Mississippi, the White Citizen's Council, a group dedicated to states' rights and preserving the "Southern Way of Life" met in preparation of the Freedom Riders' arrival in Jackson. This would become known as "White Monday" in Mississippi. The Council was determined to thwart the efforts of integration at all costs, and was keeping close tabs on the Freedom Riders. One solution would be to assemble "Minute Men" to counteract attempts made by the

SNCC and CORE to break down segregation in the south with their so-called "Freedom Rides." These Minute Men would consist of a section of the "finest" white citizens in each community who would peacefully assemble at any given point within their community to demonstrate a citizen protest against invasion from outside agitators of their institutions. It was also determined by the council that CORE was linked with conspiratorial outfits to be communist-backed. Governor Ross Barnett, determined to not have his state repeat the disaster of Alabama with Governor Patterson, decided upon another course of action. Barnett stated he "felt confident that the officers and the people could certainly handle the situation well" and that "Mississippi wasn't asking for any federal troops or marshals. In fact, he didn't want them."

On May 24th, 1961, the Freedom Riders crossed the state line into Mississippi with assistance from the federal government for protection. With wounds still freshly bandaged, the Freedom Riders passed through a densely wooded area, with forests and swamps. Mississippi National Guardsman were lined along the highway with their guns pointed toward the wooded area on either side, prepared for an ambush. Once safely through, the bus made its way towards Jackson. Upon arrival at the bus station in Jackson, no crowds were seen. Instead, police greeted the group. As the Freedom Riders unloaded the bus and sought to integrate the restrooms and waiting areas inside the station, they were told to "move along" and were led out to the other side of the building and immediately loaded into paddy wagons. The group never had the chance to challenge the facilities before they were arrested. The charges against the Freedom Riders were inciting to riot and breach of peace.

There was no rioting. No altercations or displays of violence like Alabama. James Eastland, chairman of the Senate Judiciary Committee in Mississippi, struck a deal with the Kennedy administration to keep the peace in Mississippi promising no violence. In return, the Kennedys would not enforce the federal ruling to desegregate interstate travel. However, Mississippi would have the final word, or so it thought, as to solving the problem of the Freedom Riders. To everyone else keeping a close eye on the situation, it appeared the group was doomed, and their efforts thwarted. By sending them straight to the city jail to await trial, Governor Barnett thought that "protecting" them from the white population in Mississippi would ultimately defeat them. Little did he know the Freedom Riders had adopted a strategy of "jail- no bail," and were not intimidated by the thought of being arrested. Once the jail-no bail strategy was seen in court, and the Freedom Riders refused the two-hundred dollar fine, the judge ordered them to be sent to Parchman State Penitentiary to work off the levy against them. Governor Barnett's plan was to break the back of the Freedom Riders. By sending them to Parchman, Mississippi would teach them a lesson by putting them to work.

While the first wave of Freedom Riders was on their way to Parchman in the paddy wagons, Diane Nash was already sending in fresh recruits of additional Freedom Riders with their eyes on Jackson. If Governor Barnett was determined to send the group to jail, then the Freedom Riders would now go full force with the jail-no bail strategy, and they made it their mission to fill Parchman Penitentiary to its maximum and thus overwhelm the system. In doing so, this would force Mississippi to change its policy of segregation.

Meanwhile, the first group of Freedom Riders now arriving at Parchman were booked and sent to death row to spend their time. Mississippians were kept separated from the outsiders. The cells were small and filled with many prisoners when only meant to house two. The females were kept in a different area than the males. The conditions at Parchman were designed to break a person both psychologically and physically. If the hard labor didn't get you, the psychological aspect of doing time there would. John Moody was told by a guard to answer "Yes sir or No sir" if anyone were to ask him a question, then wanted to know if he understood. Moody replied, "Yes, I understand," and was immediately hit over the head.

The Warden of Parchman, Deputy Tyson, instructed the Freedom Riders there would be no singing, praying, noise, etc. No reading material was allowed within the cells, except for the Bible. Determined to not let the time spent at Parchman get the best of them, the group would sing Freedom songs to one another from the cells. This was done for several reasons. Songs were sung along the duration of the rides as a means of solidarity- reminding everyone the purpose and goal was freedom. It helped to ease the tension and let others in the group know that by hearing the songs, everyone was alright. However, as Deputy Tyson warned, singing was not allowed. He offered a firm reprimand by telling the Freedom Riders if they kept singing, they'll be "singing in the rain." In other words, he would turn the hose on them. This didn't deter the group, and they continued to sing their songs of freedom. When the guards had enough, they would turn off the air conditioner during the day and take their mattresses away at night. This would leave the group sleeping on a cold slab of concrete. Still the singing continued, in utter defiance and as a means of a taunted warning.

"You can take my mattress Oh Yes!
You can take my mattress Oh Yes!
You can take my mattress, You can take my mattress…
You can take my mattress Oh Yes!"

When threats of removing the mattresses yet again were made to the Freedom Riders, they changed the lyrics to "You can take my mattress, Oh Yes!" Whatever Parchman was ready to dish out, the group was going to hand it back to them; determined not to allow Parchman to have the final word.

Little did the Magnolia State know the call was being answered from across the country to fill the jail cells in Jackson. When a group of Freedom Riders would arrive at the bus station, they were immediately arrested, but a second group would be right behind them. Each group still adopting the jail-no bail strategy. In the Jim Crow South, being arrested and sent to jail was the worst shame one could bear. It meant disgrace not only to yourself, but to your family. The Freedom Riders didn't see the threat of jail in this manner and instead, viewed it as a badge of honor. This was simply unheard of and unforeseen to Mississippians. The Freedom Riders exploited the weakness.

The Sovereignty Commission was also busy keeping track of the arrivals and departures at the bus stations and conducting their own investigation to keep tabs on the Freedom Riders. A report on the Freedom Riders from July 7th to July 14th of 1961 stated that a group of riders participating in a sit-in labeled "Group #24" attempted to depart Jackson on July 7th at 12:30 AM. Among this group was a young 13 year-old Hezekiah Watkins listed as "school student" at the age of fourteen and a side note of "Minnie Watkins, mother works at Primos and father is dead." There was only one problem with this in that Hezekiah wasn't allowed to be anywhere after dark, and he wasn't. Could it be that he was placed into this report grouping after being pushed into the Greyhound Station and arrested? Other reports were made during this time attesting to how Mississippi was treating the Freedom Riders with care as to protect its image as a tourist haven. Could this be part of the reason as to why Governor Ross Barnett ordered Hezekiah's release after his five day stay at Parchman Prison? Having a thirteen-year-old boy on Death Row being mixed into the wave of Freedom Riders would not denote how Mississippi was treating the Freedom Riders with care and could certainly tarnish its image if discovered.

During this time of Freedom Riders coming by the busloads into Jackson, six young Riders from Minnesota were also imprisoned at Parchman for ordering a meal from the Negro section of the Jackson bus depot. They were sentenced to four months for disturbing the peace. The parents of the jailed Freedom Riders reached out to Governor Barnett for assistance in getting to see their children. The governor of Minnesota wired Barnett about the youth and was told the parents should see a sheriff in Jackson about the matter before even attempting to contact their children. This led to the Minnesota governor instructing his Human Rights Commission to go to Jackson to take a first-hand look at the conditions of Parchman where the Freedom Riders were being held. Governor Barnett told Governor Anderson he had "some reservations" about the visit. Governor Barnett eventually agreed to the visit but made it clear he would not allow them to conduct an inspection or investigation of the jail facilities or in its handling of the Freedom Riders. Concerned with Mississippi's image, Governor Barnett allowed the visit, and the representatives from Minnesota's Human Rights Commission upheld their promise to the governor not to report on the issues of the facility and the condition of the Freedom Riders.

The overwhelming call to action left Mississippi officials in quite a predicament. Over a short amount of time, the cells at Parchman were filled to capacity. It seemed that Governor Barnett, and the Magnolia State, wasn't prepared for the resilience and determination of the Freedom Riders to challenge the Jim Crow laws of segregation. As James Farmer stated, "We felt that we could then count upon the racists of the South to create a crisis, so that the federal government would be compelled to enforce the federal law." The Freedom Rides proved this to be true. It also brought national attention, for the first time, to the Civil Rights Movement in a way unlike anything had been done before. After Jackson, Robert Kennedy petitioned the Interstate Commerce Commission for regulations banning segregation in interstate bus travel. By late September 1961, the ICC issued regulations that would allow the federal government to enforce the Supreme court ruling of Boynton vs. Virginia. The battle was won, but the war was far from over. All eyes were on the prize, and the prize was still freedom.

> *"James Bevel could do more with young people than any human being on the face of the earth."*
>
> Hosea Williams, Civil Rights Activist

pushing FORWARD

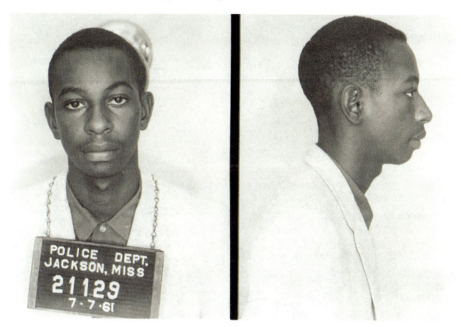

Mugshot Photo of Hezekiah Watkins, July 7, 1961
Mississippi State Sovereignty Commission File, SCRID # 2-55-5-76-1-1-1
Courtesy of Mississippi Department of Archives and History

Minnie Lee Watkins, Mother to Hezekiah

Grade school photo of Hezekiah Watkins 1955-1956

pushing FORWARD

Greyhound Bus Station in Jackson, Mississippi today.

Investigative report made of Group #24 of Freedom Riders.

Index card kept on file by the Sovereignty Commission for Hezekiah Watkins

pushing FORWARD

Top: Photo of Hezekiah as a young man

Right: Newspaper article keeping tabs on Freedom Riders arrested in Jackson. Sovereignty commission Files

Hezekiah telling his story to a group of visitors at the Mississippi Civil Rights Museum

pushing FORWARD

Flyer calling for a boycott of certain Jackson stores by John Salter and Medgar Evers. Image courtesy of Mississippi Department of Archives and History

Hezekiah pointing to his mug shot photograph at the MS Civil Rights Museum Jackson, MS

Corner Food Market and Deli owned by Hezekiah in Jackson, MS

pushing FORWARD

Dalton - Deerpark Summer Reading Enrichment Program
created by Hezekiah and his wife Chris

Area children participating in the Dalton - Deerpark Summer Enrichment Program

pushing FORWARD

Dalton - Deerpark organized the first city wide "March Against Crime" with Congressman Benny Thompson participating

Dalton - Deerpark hosts Teen Summit with speaker Judy Henry Wingate

Janet Reno speaks to Hezekiah Watkins and Brad Pigott.

pushing FORWARD

The Congressional Record for the 112th Congress, Second Session honoring Mr. Hezekiah Watkins for his service to the Jackson Community presented by Congressman Benny Thompson.

Hezekiah outside of the MS Civil Rights Museum where he works today

Hezekiah and his wife, Chris

pushing FORWARD

1) Hezekiah with his children - Marvin Lilley, Quentin Ramon and Kristi.
2) Hezekiah with his brothers - Willie (left) and O'Rell (right).   3) Hezekiah with Grandson Mason.
4) Grandson Corey.   5) Grandson Brandon.   6) Grandson "Mook" Quentin II and great grandson Kaidin.
7) Great Grandkids Kaidin and Amora Rose.   8) Hezekiah at the King Edward Hotel.
9) Hezekiah in front of Mississippi Freedom Trail Marker.

CHAPTER FIVE

Beyond the Push

The following year I attended school at Rowan, which went to the ninth grade. By this time, the principal had already talked to my mother and knew what happened at the Greyhound Bus Station. Keep in mind, this was a hush-hush thing in the community. Nobody acknowledged my involvement with the Freedom Riders. It was known to my mother that if she wanted to have her son stay in school, then nothing must be mentioned about my involvement. I could be expelled, and other bad things could happen to me or our family as a result of people knowing what happened. This was stressed to me by my mother, and I replied with a "Yes Ma'am," and that was that.

Things were good for a while. Time went by during that school year without any incident. Then, a man by the name of James Bevel started talking to me. He was a preacher, could sing, and he knew the Bible. Sometimes he would come by the house when my mother would be at work and we would go places in downtown Jackson together. At times we would walk down the street on a hot, sunny day and Bevel would say, "Well, it sure is hot! Let's get some water." I'd go directly up to the water fountain that read "Colored Only" and take a sip of water. He would let me go, but he would stand back and never get any. Bevel would point out the differences between the white's water fountain and the one for colored. The fountain for the whites to use was pristine and clean. He would then point out in contrast the one for the coloreds to use. It often had bird droppings in it and was never kept clean. On occasion you would see a white person walk up to the colored fountain and spit in it before they walked away.

On one occasion we got on a bus together. Being taught at an early age and just accepting the way of life in Mississippi, I walked directly to the back of the bus. This was where the blacks were made to sit, while the front of the bus was reserved for whites only. It was then that Bevel spoke up and said, "No. You shouldn't do that." With a confused look on my face I replied, "Well, this is where I am supposed to go." Segregation was just like knowing the right shoe or the left shoe- You knew what went where.

On another occasion, I remember being downtown with James Bevel and before long, we talked about being hungry. We started going inside Woolworth's to get a sandwich, some French-fries, and a Coke. I told Bevel, "No. I'm not going in there. I'm going to go around to the back. That's where we're supposed to go. We need to go to the back to get what we want to order, but I'm not going inside." James Bevel always made it a mission to point out injustices on these trips around the city. To this day I'm not sure if I was more afraid of being arrested again or of my Momma finding out and giving me another beatdown for doing what I was doing. I thought to myself that I didn't want my mother getting onto me again, and I'm not going to deal with James Bevel telling me to do these things that could possibly get me into trouble. But things wouldn't end that easily with Bevel.

There was one thing every kid in our neighborhood looked forward to, and that was my mother's Bible study she hosted at our house every Wednesday. She would prepare snacks for the neighborhood kids, and everyone would gather in our living room. It was always packed with children! She would always encourage all the kids to study and bring their Bible, and then they could participate in the activities during the Bible Study (and of course, enjoy the food). My Mom was the head chef at Primo's restaurant, and the restaurant would allow her to take home pastries or other items that didn't sell that day. My mother, not believing in throwing away food, would often serve the food for our weekly Bible study. I'm not sure if the kids were really into the Bible so much, or the fact my mother was giving away snacks.

One night, James Bevel decided to show up at my house for one of these weekly Bible Studies. He wasn't going to give up on me so quickly, and he began showing up more regularly. After a while of doing this, Bevel just sort of took over. He came up with the idea of calling out a chapter and a verse and seeing who could turn to it the fastest. If they read a couple of lines, then the person would win a prize. My mother enjoyed this because it brought in more neighborhood kids, and they were learning about the Bible. It was a good thing. At one point there came a time when we didn't have enough room in our house with all the kids participating in the Bible Study. There was nowhere for them to sit.

All of this seemed great, but I had no idea what was going on in terms of James Bevel's plan. What he was really doing was trying to recruit me in order to draw in other teenagers. The thing was… no one knew it. I didn't know. My mother didn't know. The kids didn't know. I'm sure my mother thought at the time, "Here is this man doing something good for the Lord." She probably thought he would convert a lot of the kids, and they would stop doing whatever bad things it was they were doing at the time.

On Sundays, we would all go to church and have a good time praising the Lord. I remember one Sunday James Bevel got up and befriended the pastor of our church. The pastor even gave him permission to preach. When Bevel gave his sermon, he didn't preach anything about Civil Rights. What he did keep saying was, "Oh Lord, save the children!" With that, he won over the pastor, and the congregation. And of course, he'd already won over my mother. So, with James Bevel came my first real push into the Movement as an official Freedom Rider.

In 1962, I had just begun my journey when Medgar Evers asked blacks to not go to the Mississippi State Fair. During this time, whites would have a whole week to enjoy the fair's festivities. When their time was over, the blacks had only three days. By then, most of the rides had been taken down and moved on to the next stop. It was frustrating to the blacks not to have the same number of days or the same rides as the whites.

A bunch of students that week decided to go to the fair during the week that was designated for whites. We wanted to experience the fair the same way they did and have a chance to enjoy all of the rides. While out walking around on the fairgrounds, a few police officers noticed us. They had dogs with them, and once they saw us, they decided to let the dogs loose on us! We took off and the dogs started running wild behind us.

One of the students with us ran track at Lanier High School. His name was Ralph Floyd, and he was one of the fastest runners around. To this day, I don't think his record has ever been broken. Ralph took off and ran so fast that he left us behind. The dogs, in pursuit of him, ran right past us and after Ralph. I knew it was because of this that our lives had just been spared. I don't think the police officers could've made it to us in time, and even if they wanted to, they wouldn't have pulled the dogs off us.

Ralph continued running, with the dogs in pursuit after him all the way past the fairgrounds and towards State Street. When the light was green, southbound, Ralph ran so fast he ran through the light where he was supposed to stop with oncoming traffic. The cars had the right of way. Ralph made it through the traffic, but the police dogs didn't. The next day, the report on the incident stated that one of the police dogs was killed by us. Ralph was accused of killing the dog intentionally, but we all knew this wasn't the case because we saw it with our own eyes.

In the community where I grew up, almost all the males were participating in the Movement. The following May, when I was in high school at Lanier, about eighty percent of the students were involved. I remember how we did a walkout to protest a variety of things. First, we wanted better textbooks. The white students received the newest and updated textbooks at their school. When they would receive new textbooks, we would get their hand-me-downs, which we old and falling apart with pages torn out that had been written in. Another issue we protested was the quality of the food in our school. All of these reasons led us to the decision of walking out.

On the day the walkout was to take place, word spread throughout the community and we even had two other schools to join. The students worked hard to organize and plan the walkout. We ended up with about ninety-five percent of the entire student body participating. The amazing thing was it was completely done by the students without any help from the major organizations associated with the Movement. I don't think anyone with CORE, SNCC, the NAACP, or the mayor thought we could organize something like this without their leadership. But we did.

The next day, close to five hundred students from three high schools marched towards Farish Baptist Church, where the NAACP held their mass meetings. The police arrested the first group of marchers, numbering approximately seventy-five students, and later arrested the remaining group as they made their way towards Capitol Street. The police quickly realized there was a problem of having no place to store everyone, since the jails were full, so they decided to use the fairgrounds as a means to hold us. However, second problem arose in how they were going to transport us without having enough vehicles. The solution they came up with was garbage trucks. So, we were transported to the Fairgrounds by means of these garbage trucks, with trash and debris that we were made to stand in. Once we made it to the Fairgrounds, we were put into the area where they normally kept the livestock. Then we had to deal with the manure, and sleep on the floor. They brought cots or mattresses by, so you either got a cot or mattress, but then you had to find a suitable place to put it. I remember choosing a cot so I could at least be off the ground. All of this was done as a means to disgrace us.

No one outside of us students knew this was going to happen. Not even our parents. It was just a word of mouth type of thing. It wasn't sanctioned by any of the organizations. We just did it. Everybody had to stay at the Fairgrounds overnight. The police didn't let anyone go until the following day and even then, there were only a few of us who they let go. The rest of us remained at the Fairgrounds. There are misconceptions that Freedom Riders were held at the Fairgrounds, but they weren't. These were local students.

There were students who chose not to get involved in the Movement and did so for their own reasons. One reason was as simple as the fact we didn't have our own playgrounds in the neighborhood. If we wanted to play, we had to go to the playground at the neighborhood school. If someone was at the school when the police rode by and happened to see a person who might have been arrested with the student protesters or Freedom Riders, they would make everyone go home. Then the neighborhood kids had nowhere to play and they would hate on us by saying, "Just because of you, I can't play now!" Sometimes it would turn into a verbal disagreement; however, this sometimes led to a physical altercation with people who were mad at us just because we were there. Because of this, not everyone was willing to get involved.

We knew the price we would have to pay with becoming a Freedom Rider. It would come at a great cost to those who were local. We caught more of a setback during this time than the ones who came in because those Freedom Riders, when released from jail, had a place to stay or could go back home. We, however, had to stay here in Jackson and deal with many setbacks and consequences that our friends from outside states didn't have to face. Not only was there an issue with the police, but we had to live in this community. The neighborhood stores, which were all owned by white merchants, got to where they didn't want to serve us. It eventually got so bad we found ourselves catching it from all angles. The worst of it being when my mother lost her job as head chef at Primos due to my involvement with the Freedom Riders.

During the Movement, the White Citizens Council kept a list of all the activities of black citizens in the community and kept a close eye on everything- even down to the food you ordered from certain restaurants. If you were black and lost your job, there was no way you could recover. Your property or home would be foreclosed. Individuals who were renting from whites were evicted for no reason. The Citizens Council infiltrated every part of the community. These were the kinds of things that were happening all the time, and the kinds of troubles we were continually faced with.

When word got out I was involved in The Movement, my mother lost her job. I now found myself with a new kind of trouble on my hands; I had to face my unemployed mother on a regular basis, knowing I was the reason she was not working. My brother, Willie, would often comment years down the road the reason I ended up getting arrested so many times was because I didn't want to be at home. Maybe he was right.

One day a white man in a big car was driving slowly down our street and stopped in front of our house. My brother was outside at the time when the man rolled down his window and asked, "Does Minnie Watkins stay here?"

My brother O'Rell, being somewhat of a radical, was unafraid and replied to the man, "What do you mean does Minnie Watkins stay here? You don't come by here calling my Momma by her name, Minnie Watkins. You don't know her."

"I'm sorry," replied the man. "Mrs. Watkins. Does she stay here?"

"Yeah," replied my brother. "Who are you? What do you want with my mother?"

As it turned out, the white man was Mr. Smith, a regular who had been eating at Primos restaurant for a long time who was now contemplating opening a new restaurant. When he found out my mother was fired, he hurried to track her down to recruit her for his business.

"I want to talk to her about a job," replied Mr. Smith. It was then that all the radical/meanness and hate just went away in my brother, with his entire expression changing instantly. With a big smile on his face he then replied, "Oh, Yes Sir! Yes Sir! I'll get her. Stay right here, Sir. Don't you leave. I'm coming right back, Sir!"

My mother then came out of the house, following my brother, and the man introduced himself. I remember thinking to myself, "Oh yes! Thank you, Jesus!" Even though the new restaurant was not yet open, he asked my mother if she could be there at a certain time. She didn't seem too enthused by everything but said, "Okay." It would be a month before the restaurant opened, but he told my mother he wanted her there the next day. Mr. Smith wanted my mother to make an inventory list of everything that needed to be done and he would take care of the rest. That was one of the good things that came out of it all. I was happy for my mother, and I was happy for me. I even drove her there the following day.

It wasn't long after this incident I was sent to Canton, Mississippi. I began helping with voter registration and desegregation in the surrounding areas. This was a fun time for me, and I found the work to be enjoyable.

From Canton, I was then sent to Greenwood and Greenville in the Delta. Again, I was involved in helping with voter registration and desegregation. I would be dropped off, attempt to desegregate a place, and get arrested. Upon my release, I'd do the same thing. One arrest here, another arrest there. It didn't matter. I was involved in something I felt was making a difference.

During this time, I experienced the worst beating I've ever had. I was in Canton with a friend of mine named Lawrence Guyot. The two of us were in a vehicle together when we were stopped by the police. One of the officers was the sheriff of Madison County. When asking us questions, Lawrence kept replying with a yes and no answer. That's when the sheriff told him to say, "Yes, Sir." Lawrence refused. It was then the Sheriff called for other officers to come where we were. When they arrived, they proceeded to beat Lawrence. I kept telling myself "Lawrence, please. Please say yes, sir," but he wouldn't. They beat him until he collapsed. Then they started on me. I'm telling you, I started saying "Yes sir" right then and there. One officer asked me a question and turned in my direction. The only thing I could say was "Yes, sir, Yes, sir."

When I wasn't in Canton, I was back in Jackson almost every weekend. Medgar Evers was playing an active role as the field secretary for the NAACP and leading boycott protests of certain stores. We, as the Youth of the NAACP, at first weren't pleased with a lot of what Medgar was doing. Roy Wilkins, the Executive Director for the NAACP, didn't want Medgar out front playing any public role. He just wanted him doing speaking engagements to raise money. That was it. I believe it was Roy who asked Medgar to back off; suggesting he was doing too much. The NAACP was there for legal guidance and to raise money to post bail for those arrested, or to handle whatever kind of injustices that had been handed down to someone. Medgar wasn't sitting on the sidelines, and that's when the youth really started to back him.

Things did not happen, that I know of, with his life being threatened until he became actively involved. As long as he was speaking here or there, I assumed everything was going well until he began to lead demonstrations. We boycotted the A&P and blocked the entrance to the store, and we wouldn't let blacks in who were trying to get in to shop. I remember the manager calling the police.

When the police came, we opened a small gap so they could go in. Medgar led several of those types of demonstrations. Most of them were organized by him. We were happy to follow his lead.

The night Medgar was assassinated, I was passing out flyers announcing the mass meeting he would be speaking at, which was held at a church named, New Jerusalem on Whitfield Street. We were passing out flyers when we saw Medgar arrive. I was given a little twenty-two pistol and was told to ride up and down the perimeter of the church, and to report any suspect, or any person that wasn't supposed to be there, either black or white. How were we gonna tell if he was black and not supposed to be there? I didn't know. I was told not to shoot anyone with the pistol, and that it was for my safety. If I spotted anything unusual, I was to come back and let a guy named Jesse Davis know. We didn't spot anything unusual that night, and that was that. I didn't get a chance to hear Medgar Evers speak that night, and after he left, I assumed he went directly home.

The next day, it was in the afternoon before the news really got around that he had been assassinated. This was devastating to the entire community. We thought Medgar had begun to move in and do the things we felt needed to be done.

After Medgar's death, we had others to come in and see what they could do, and it became a parade of confusion. Everybody was trying to come in and be the next person, but no one could do what Medgar did. The only organization that had stability to move in and help was the SCLC. Wherever Dr. King went, he drew a crowd. Ella Baker was the one person who was able to pull all of those organizations together. She was well known in all of the organizations and was something like a spokesperson for all of them. When there was something like an argument, she stepped in between and said, "Let's do it like this," and it was just that way. People listened to her.

Medgar always reminded us the importance of nonviolence, even when our anger and frustrations grew. He knew the way to get where we needed to go was by remaining nonviolent. When he died, we found ourselves lacking in leadership.

It's important to note that although there was the noble cause on the part of the Freedom Riders to challenge segregation, there were a lot of young folks who became Freedom Riders for different reasons. Some were already in some sort of trouble and either had warrants for their arrest or were possibly rebelling against their parents. Others just wanted to get the hell out of the city or state they were in, and this was a free ride. Some of the Freedom Riders felt this way: What can we do? We don't have money, and I want to go someplace… Where can I go? The answer was Mississippi, not thinking of the fear you could lose your life by going. The police were suspicious of anyone, be it an outside agitator or local person, who was involved with any organization.

*"The gifts of God should be enjoyed
by all citizens in Mississippi."*

Medgar Evers

pushing FORWARD

CHAPTER SIX

A Call to Action in Jackson

In Jackson, the call for desegregation was being heard loud and clear by the black community. Jackson's total population included 250,000 residents. 50,000 of its black citizens were determined to wipe out segregation in every aspect around the city. This included public facilities, parks, playgrounds, libraries, schools, lunchrooms, lunch counters, and to remove all segregations signs. On the agenda was also the push to hire more blacks on the police force, upgrade the salaries of black municipal workers, and to form a biracial committee.

By September of 1962, the Supreme Court upheld James Meredith's admission to attend Ole Miss, to which Governor Ross Barnett started to a televised audience "There is no case in history where the Caucasian race has survived social integration." He further added that the state of Mississippi "Will not drink from the cup of genocide." Federal marshals had attempted to register Meredith, unsuccessfully, a total of four times. A compromise was reached by Barnett and Attorney General, Robert Kennedy, and on the night of September 30th, over one hundred federal marshals, close to three hundred border patrolmen and approximately one hundred federal prison guards secretly escorted Meredith on campus. However, the attempt was not without retaliation. A mob numbering close to two thousand people attacked the marshals and an all-out brawl ensued, which forced Kennedy's hand to send in federal troops. By 8 o'clock the following morning, Meredith was successfully registered at Ole Miss, making him the first black student to register successfully.

With Meredith now enrolled, a continuous effort was made by members of SNCC to register voters, particularly in Greenwood, Mississippi. Medgar Evers was especially inspired during a visit to the Delta to see the efforts taking place there. If people were making significant progress in a place like Greenwood, then there should be no reason why the same efforts couldn't be made back in Jackson. This was the turning point in Medgar's decision to become more directly involved in furthering the Movement back home. It required direct action, much to the disapproval of the NAACP, causing Medgar to reexamine his commitment to the organization.

Meanwhile, back in Jackson, Youth Council Members, mentored by John Salter, started printing the "North Jackson Action" newsletter. The first plan of action was to boycott the Mississippi State Fair later that October. During this time, the whites had a full week to enjoy the festivities of the fair. This included all the rides, attractions, and food. At the end of the week, the remaining three days were designated for the blacks to go to the fair. By this time, as Hezekiah stated, most of the rides were in the process of being taken down. The black citizens of Jackson never got the opportunity to experience the Mississippi State Fair in all its glory leading to only three percent of blacks participating in the fair that year.

The second plan of action called for a boycott of stores along Capitol Street and would begin in November. Together, John Salter and Medgar Evers created four goals for the boycott:
- Equality in hiring and promotion
- The end of segregated drinking fountains, restrooms and seating.
- Use of courtesy titles: Mrs., Miss, and Mr.
- Service on a first-come, first-served basis

Leaflets were printed and distributed, listing specific stores or businesses on Capitol Street to boycott which promoted segregation. It was strongly urged that all black citizens participate in the boycott and support the movement.

John Salter, who was hard at work, along with his wife and four Tougaloo students, decided to picket in front of Woolworth's retail store. Woolworth's was a popular five and dime store and was a twentieth-century fixture of downtown Americana. It served as a common staple for retail in addition to an affordable meal at their lunch counters. It was also common practice in the Jim Crow South for these lunch counters to be segregated. The boycott included Woolworth's, in addition to a good many other businesses on Capitol Street who practiced segregation. During the picketing, close to fifty police officers showed up and the group was arrested. Thus began the first arrests for the campaign. From December to April of the following year, the boycott of Jackson businesses continued with a participation rate ranging from 65-90 % of the black citizens.

On May 28th, 1963, the Woolworth's in Jackson was once again the attention of the campaign. This time, John Salter and his students from Tougaloo College would not be moved. A sit-in was planned that day to protest the segregated lunch counters. Three students, Anne Moody, Memphis Norman, Pearlena Lewis, along with Salter, sat at the "Whites Only" lunch counter at Woolworth's in an attempt at desegregation. Although the integration of the counter itself was present through the students, no one would wait on them due to strict instructions to not serve any blacks. After some time, Central High School released for lunch and the crowds began to grow. The students, looking for their own kind of action, began shouting out obscenities and taunting the students. Before long, the verbal assaults escalated to physical violence, as the students had condiments poured on top of their heads and Norman was pulled from his stool at the counter. He was punched and kicked until bloodied. Police officers stood by passively and watched as the event unfolded right before them. After the violence continued for a good amount of time, the officers finally broke it up and arrested Memphis Norman.

Joan Trumpauer Mulholland filled Norman's empty seat and next Anne and Peralena. Determined to desegregate the lunch counter, even amidst the brutality and violence that was displayed to them, the students remained in their positions. The sit-in continued for hours until the manager of the store decided to close it down. The president of Tougaloo College, Dr. A.D. Beittel, heard of the incident and arrived at the store to escort the students out, due to the stationary mob lurking outside. As the students were escorted from the store, a line of policemen held back the mob from getting to them. Although the line contained the angry mob, it didn't keep the officers from throwing the items collected in the frenzy at the students.

The Woolworth's Lunch Counter Sit-in of 1963 was the catalyst that set off a blaze within the Movement in Jackson. Through the North Jackson Action Newsletter, Salter now gained greater attention to the Jackson NAACP resulting in more funding and recognized attention and support for SNCC and CORE.

The events of the Woolworth's Sit-in led to close to 500 students from area high schools, including Hezekiah's school; Lanier, to participate in a mass march adopting the jail-no-bail strategy for those who would be arrested. The students began their march out of the Farish Baptist Church, exiting in pairs. Carrying American flags, the marchers were met by hundreds of cops and whites in cars, prowling the city with confederate flags. The police barricaded the street and even started beating some of the marchers with clubs. By the time they were done, most of the 500 students were arrested. It was decided the animal stockade at the fairgrounds would be used as a holding facility to detain them all. The mode to transport all these students? Not a paddy wagon, but garbage trucks! To add insult to injury, the black citizens of Jackson were being held as prisoners on the same fairgrounds they were never allowed equal access to. If you're a visitor to the Civil Rights Museum in Jackson, be sure to take note if you walk out the back entrance of the museum to the parking garage at the vast, empty ground directly in front of you. You will be looking at the very site of the fairgrounds which once held the student protestors.

The efforts of protest and boycott in Jackson were met with equal opposition and at times it seemed like a tug-of-war match between the two opposing sides. For every advance made by everyone involved with the campaign, the white citizens of Jackson pushed back in their own way. On June 6th, 1963 Hinds County Court issued an injunction against all forms of Movement activity, determined to cripple their efforts. Even though the injunction violates the protected rights of free speech and assembly, the National NAACP leaders came to a decision not to defy the ruling. The boycott had proven to be effective but the local business owners did not dare go against the power of the White Citizens Council to hire blacks for their establishments. Previous efforts were made by NAACP Field Secretary, Medgar Evers, and other leaders in the Movement to meet with Mayor Allen Thompson to meet the demands established in the campaign. The Jackson mayor agreed to meet with only a select few black leaders and promised to desegregate public facilities, as well as to hire a few black cops, only to deny them later.

On June 12th, 1963 Medgar Evers attended a mass meeting at the New Jerusalem Church on Foothill Street in Jackson. The meeting lasted long into the night, and Hezekiah was given the task of patrolling the church for any suspicious person. The meeting came to an end, and with nothing out of the normal activity to report, everyone dispersed and made their way home. Medgar Evers did the same. Tired and ready to be home with his family, he pulled into the driveway of his house and got out of his car. Little did he know that a White Supremacist named Byron De la Beckwith, was hiding in the bushes nearby. With the pull of a trigger, a shot was fired, hitting Medgar in the back. Bloodied and wounded, Medgar managed to make his way to the doorstep in his garage where his wife, Myrlie, and their three small children watched in horror as he took his last breath.

Medgar had long caught the attention of the Citizen's Council. Being a believer in equal voting rights and an advocate of boycotting businesses owned by whites, along with playing an active role in leading many of these protests, he was on the radar of people in the black community being heavily monitored. Byron De la Beckwith, who as eager to fit in to the prominent white society, was willing to carry out the task of what the whites felt would be "doing the community a favor" in getting rid of him.

Beckwith would be apprehended shortly after the assassination. The gun he used was found with his fingerprints on the weapon. However, confident in his alibi of two eyewitnesses, both white policemen, who "saw" him in Greenwood that evening, Beckwith set out for trial. Beckwith was equally confident in the fact that no all-white jury in Mississippi would convict him of a crime, even if it was murder, with him being a white man. He was tried and acquitted twice; each time with an all-white jury. During one of the trials, the former governor, Ross Barnett, was even seen shaking hands with Beckwith, as he stood by his side. It wouldn't be until February 5, 1994- some thirty years after the assassination, that Byron De la Beckwith would be found guilty and sentenced to life in jail. The case was reopened due to work by Jerry Mitchell, who was with the Clarion Ledger researching files from the Mississippi State Sovereignty Commission. Even then Beckwith was quoted as saying, "I'm proud of my enemies. They're every color but white, every creed but Christian."

The murder of Medgar Evers shook the foundations of the heart of the Civil Rights Movement in Jackson to its core. The black community had suffered a tremendous loss and now found themselves without a leader to guide them. Medgar was a tender, soft-spoken soul who believed firmly in the principle that nonviolence was the answer to solving the injustices faced in Mississippi. He led by example and was quick to remind others that violence was not the solution. With tensions high, and a community devasted and rocked to its core, the exact opposite of everything Medgar stood for took place the day of his funeral as things took a violent turn for the worse. People were angry and unsure of which direction to go without Medgar's leadership. It signified the beginning of uncertain times within the Movement as many attempted to step up and fill the role of leadership that was now lacking. The only problem was, Medgar Evers was one in a million and no one could adequately fill his shoes.

*"The road to freedom must be uphill,
even if it is arduous and frustrating."*

Andrew Goodman

pushing FORWARD

CHAPTER SEVEN

Freedom Summer and Beyond

The summer of 1964 had arrived and along with it were student activists from across the country who occupied every city and town in Mississippi, wanting to register the black community to vote. Most of my time during Freedom Summer was spent in Greenville talking to people and telling them to vote while providing information to help them register. Most of them did not understand the power of the right to vote.

One of the great things that came from that summer was the formation of the Freedom Democratic Party. It was only at this point that people realized that if we could get blacks registered to vote, then we could do something to really change things. We all saw how much attention the Freedom Riders received, and now the focus was on voter registration. I personally didn't know a lot about the process of registering to vote, or the importance of being a registered voter. After attending several classes conducted by the students, I learned a lot about the political process and the officials. It was an experience I really enjoyed. Once it began to make sense to me, I was then able to go out and spread the news with others to get them to go to the courthouse.

There were a lot of tactics used to prevent a person from voting, particularly in the Delta. The whites knew the importance and power behind the vote and they went to great lengths to prevent blacks from having access to this right. There were a few people I personally took to register at the courthouse and heard them asking the person, "Tell me how many pennies are in this jar?" Sometimes the tax collector would come up with something along the lines of, "How high can Joe jump?" I recall getting my mother registered in Jackson and she didn't have to go through this, but many others did.

I would tell applicants to be at the courthouse no later than 8 am, because it would open at nine for voter registration, and we wanted to make sure they were up early before the property owners arrived. We wanted to get in there and get out as quickly as possible.

While at the courthouse, a sheriff deputy would walk through with a gun on his hip. It was a tactic of intimidation. Once we were there, many older applicants would get inside and be scared to death to proceed. They would change their mind based on the deputy looking over their shoulder and following them around. Then a lot of times they would trail you all the way to where you were going, and that's how we lost a lot of people. They would say, "The heck with it! I'm not even gonna worry with it." It was the younger folks that got things going. When they were old enough to register, they did. They were not intimidated the way the older folks were.

There were many times we feared for our lives and would try to take certain precautions, such as not being on a dirt road by yourself, especially at night. Even during the day, if you heard a truck coming down a dirt road, regardless of whether it was facing you or behind you, the intentions were never known or what would be going through the driver's mind. You never knew if that day would be your last. Those were all ways to intimidate you, and I'll tell you… I was intimidated many times. I was scared.

Both the student activists who came to Mississippi that summer, and the local activists, stayed in a place we called, "The Freedom House." It was a big house with several rooms. Each room, on average, would accommodate 10 to 12 individuals. We all had sleeping bags and some folks in the community would stay up all night guarding The Freedom House to help protect us. I would go outside on occasion to smoke cigarettes, since smoking inside wasn't allowed. Some of us would go out there and have conversations with the community folks who sat there on guard with their shotguns. They never did shoot anyone, and during my time there, no one ever shot or harmed any of us. The locals in the community welcomed us and were ready to defend us, if needed.

One thing that's never talked about with Freedom Summer is how there was a lot of sexual conduct going on. White males and black females…White females and black males… I've often been asked if I engaged in anything while there. The answer is no. I was too young, but there was a lot of it in each town and city. Many of the college students were already engaged in sexual conduct, so it was happening although no one seems to talk about it. My Momma used to say, "If you haven't had it, then you don't have to worry about it. You only worry about it once you've had it. Then you have to have it." The white guys were more interested in the black females. Maybe it was because there were more males here than females. I don't know.

One would think the White Citizens Council would have known what was going on in those Freedom Houses, with blacks and whites living together. There was little to no furniture in these big rooms and you would have all these young folks, black and white, staying in the same place. You also could never tell who was going to be spending the night because you had so many people coming into Jackson. There might be a group coming in from Greenville or Clarksdale to spend the night and that's just where they'd be. There were always plenty of sleeping bags and cots but the thing was, you just never knew the number that was going to be there.

To my knowledge, those Freedom Houses were never burned, bombed, or had a cross burned in front of them. The Freedom House in Jackson had a big porch and there were 15 to 20 people out on the porch at one time. It was located on the corner of Pearl and Rose, and whites passed through there all the time. The House sat in the middle of a black community. Still, that didn't stop the Klan from their activity with other houses. I recall there being a grill on the outside and at times, we would have barbeque and music to keep things lively. Everybody had a great time.

One great thing to come out of Freedom Summer was the creation of "Freedom

Schools." I remember transporting kids to a little church that was turned into a school. On certain days I would take the kids to a vacant lot with a big tree where they would have class. The student activists, many of whom were white, had an entire curriculum they were teaching the community children. They taught and exposed the kids to a number of different subjects, and the kids took to it quickly. Subjects included Advanced Algebra, Geometry and African-American Literature that were not taught in black schools during that time. The subject matter taught in local schools only focused on reading, writing and basic arithmetic. These kids never had a white person teaching them anything, and I remember how attentive they were based on these young college students standing before them and teaching them these subjects. They started adapting to their style of teaching and learned very quickly. Once their regular school started, these children were more advanced because of the college students who had taught them. Most people never talk about the content of the schools and the impact it had on those individuals, but it was life changing for them. I know it was also life changing for me.

After my senior year in high school, I wanted to keep doing what I was doing within The Movement and didn't want to go to college. For the most part, it was a good life. I was traveling to New York, California and other places and eating well! I didn't want any part of going to school. However, my mother had other plans. She kept calling me and calling me to come home. When I finally went home to Jackson in September 1965, my mother stated she wanted me to go to Jackson State University. Now, I already knew the time for registration had already passed, but she still insisted. When she found out for herself the deadline for registration had passed, I laughed and thought to myself, "See! I told you so!"

Of course, this was short-lived as a lady who knew my mother told her I could get in at Utica Junior College and they would accept me. After being prodded by my mother, I went to the campus and registered. Come to think of it, I don't believe I was even asked for my transcript. My time on campus also included my continued participation in The Movement. I was there with Congressman Benny Thompson and we were trying to get students registered to become voters. I recall one day how we were called into the President's office with a group of other students, and we were told we needed to stop trying to register the students to vote or else we would be kicked out. We might have stopped for a minute but were back at it in no time.

One day, while sitting in class, there was a knock on the door. The teacher went to open it and standing there were two military police. After several minutes of talking to them, the teacher pointed in my direction. I heard one of them look at me and said, "Watkins!"

With a puzzled expression on my face, I thought to myself, "What do you want with me?" Nothing else was said other than, "Come with us."

Not having any idea what was going on, I got up from my desk and followed the two men outside.

He said, "Get your belongings. You've been inducted into the Armed Forces."

Just like that, I was then taken to Jackson where they did the processing and paperwork. I had no choice in the matter. Back then, people could do this sort of thing and get away with it. After the paperwork was completed, I was sent to Fort Polk, Louisiana the same day for training. From there, I was sent to South Korea. I knew instantly this was not for me and had to get out. So, I left and went to Milwaukee, Wisconsin, thinking no one would find me. I was wrong. When I was located by the Armed Forces, I wasn't court marshaled but we came to an understanding that I would go back and finish my time and not let this happen again. So I did.

After my time served and once I was back home, I picked up where I left off with The Movement. It wasn't long before the arrests began to add up. A protest here, a demonstration there. In total, my arrest record numbered over 100 including an occasion when I was arrested with Dr. Martin Luther King Jr. A lot of us, including Dr. King, were put into a large cell together; like a holding facility. The thing that I'll always remember about Dr. King was how he kept up our morale by telling a lot of jokes. He kept us laughing. Before we knew it, we were all joking about our situation. He kept us going and it was enjoyable. Our minds were on him, and not on being stuck in jail. I was also arrested with Stokely Carmichael, founder of the Black Power Movement.

One of the scariest experiences of my life took place in May 1967 near the campus of Jackson State University. Lynch Street went right through the college. There was a red light there, and whites would come through that part of campus and throw things out of their cars; including half-filled or empty beer cans while they waited on the light to turn green. Sometimes these objects would hit us and while I wasn't there the first night this happened, I was told this is what started everything.

One evening, a group of guys retaliated at the white motorists by throwing rocks. Then, someone called the police. By the time the police got there, everybody was gone. The news got out when this happened and a group of us decided to go check things out. We were near the campus, maybe a block away, when the highway patrolmen, sheriff and police officers came with their firearms. White motorists claimed someone had shot them. This is when the police began shooting. They said it only lasted a for a few seconds, however, it felt much longer.

I was with my girlfriend and we ran towards a nearby cemetery. She and I both took cover in the graveyard and ducked behind one of the headstones. I recall quite vividly the bullets hitting the concrete headstone that night. That was the only thing that saved us. We had to lie flat on the grave in order to avoid being shot. My girlfriend ended up being shot in the hip with shotgun pellets. It was a long time before we were able to leave from behind the headstone, and we were afraid to breathe, much less move. A friend of mine, Ben Brown, was the only person that was killed that night. He didn't die at the scene, but he did pass away at the hospital. That experience has stayed with me throughout my life.

As time went by, I never gave up my dedication of pursuing equality. This came about in many different ways. The experiences I lived through challenged me to want to make a difference any way I possibly could. Eventually, the opportunity for me to run for office for a city council position presented itself, and I decided to pursue it. No one knew better than me the area in the district I was running for. When it came time for campaigning, I didn't need to do that much. Everyone in the neighborhood was pulling for me, and even ended up coming to me for my campaign signs to place in their yards. I ended up making the run off in the election, and I was incredibly excited! It had been a very close election and as anyone running for office of any kind can tell you, there's a lot of heart and soul that's placed into a campaign. I ended up losing in the run off.

After the run off, an older Civil Rights activist in the area came to me and told me I needed to go to the election commission and ask them to wait before they declared a winner in the election. Confused by what I was hearing, I asked, "Why?" The response was that it was discovered that dead people had apparently voted in the election and this could be proven. When I heard this, I went straight to the election commission and told them the information that was told to me. They held the election results for several weeks to investigate further. The decision was finally made to proceed with the certified votes because they claimed there was no proof despite the contrary. However, the commission stated that since they couldn't get the individuals to say they voted, "Your opponent will say they voted for you and you're saying they voted for your opponent." I was told by certain political officials to drop the matter because I could possibly create problems for others down the line. I was devastated. My political career, and hopes of making a difference in that way, was over. When you lose an election, it takes so much out of you. After all of this, I was hurt for a long time, but I never gave up my ambition to make things better around me. I just found different ways of doing so.

"Never forget where we came from, and always praise the bridges that carried us over."

Fannie Lou Hamer

pushing FORMWARD

CHAPTER EIGHT

Pursuing Equality

It was a radical idea, and one that was just crazy enough to possibly work. The idea behind the Mississippi Freedom Summer Project (sponsored by CORE and SNCC) was to infiltrate every small town and city in the state of Mississippi with an influx of eager students from across the country whose purpose was to register as many African-Americans in Mississippi to vote.

However, it was met with some reservation within the black community. Many folks were concerned that by having a bunch of publicity from whites being involved, it would defeat the grass-roots effort local organizations had put into place and were making an effort to grow.

The black community wasn't the only one suspicious of the project. With the wave of outside-agitators flooding the state during the Freedom Rides, Mississippi was on guard to what they considered to be another threat with the incoming students trying to stir up trouble and change the way of life in their state. As a matter of fact, no one really knew what to think of these new "Freedom Riders" as most would refer to them. The white community didn't want to have any part in their way of life being disturbed, and they were prepared to protect things in the state by all means necessary.

A number of monumental events happened leading to the events of the Mississippi Freedom Summer Project. After the murder of Medgar Evers, in

August 1963, countless people participated in the March on Washington to advocate for civil and economic rights for the black community. That following September, a bombing took place by the Klan at Sixteenth Street Baptist Church in Birmingham, resulting in four children being killed; Denise McNair, Carole Robertson, Addie Mae Collins, and Cynthia Wesley. The four girls had just completed their Sunday School lesson and were in the basement of the church changing into choir robes when the bomb struck out of nowhere. It was a truly horrifying event, upsetting people across the country. In November of the same year, the nation found itself in shock and would weep at the assassination of President John F. Kennedy in Dallas, TX.

Mississippi held firm in its dedicated efforts to segregation and preserving its treasured way of life. A backlash was now rising in the state, resulting from the gains being made nationally, and Mississippi would have no part of it. It was decided the influx of outside agitators was seen as an invasion and would be met with swift action. However, this did not deter the students determined to come into the state who were compelled to make a difference.

When the students first arrived in their assigned towns and cities in Mississippi, the first issue they quickly discovered was having no place to stay. Since they were not welcomed by the white community in the state and were seen as a threat from up north, the students were welcomed into the homes of people within the black community. Many students found this to be an enlightening experience. It was an opportunity to be completely immersed into the culture and to get a good feel of Mississippi and its people they had set out to help. Within the black community, it was met at first with a sense of uneasiness. Unsure of interactions with white people, many of the black families who took in students would answer with a "Yes Ma'am" or "No Sir," while looking downward. The deeply-rooted instincts and mannerisms of segregation, which had been forced upon them throughout generations was not easily broken. Students were aware of this to some degree, and they made adjustments in their interactions such as sitting and not standing over the black residents, as to not give the impression of an aggressive white person.

Whites and blacks cohabitating together was completely radical and unheard of in Mississippi. Mississippi was a state whose dedication to maintaining segregation, found itself in a situation where segregation was more or less now being forced upon everyone. It was an invasion of "mongralization," as many would put it. The Mississippi Summer Freedom Project would not be successful if its white citizens had any say in it. Mayor Allen Thompson of Jackson, in response to these outside invaders, made the decision to double his police force and introduced an armored tank dubbed the "Thompson Tank" to serve as a means to put a stop to the invasion at all costs, fully supported by tax payer's money of course (including its black citizens of whom the tank would be used against). All efforts were in full effect, and the whites of Mississippi were ready.

Students were aware of the potential violence, especially in the Magnolia State. It was something that continually stayed on everyone's mind day in and day out. Certain safety precautions were taken, such as staying in groups, being aware of one's surroundings at all times, and not being out after dark. Role play was something students participated in with preparation for potential violence they might encounter. Certain scenarios would be acted out, such as what to do if encountering a mob or if attacked while remaining nonviolent; a principle at the heart of both SNCC and CORE, and well-practiced by the Freedom Rides.

Despite the dangers, the students went on with their mission and a number of effective initiatives were implemented with the volunteers. One of them was the establishment of Freedom Schools. The concept of the Freedom Schools was to expose children in the black community to quality education that had been lacking in the state due to segregation. The make-do schools were set up in whatever places were available in convenient in location. The students derived a curriculum that was unlike anything they had ever experienced before. For the first time, they were exposed to black history and literature. The students taught them advanced math and for the first time, they were encouraged to express their views/thoughts, and listened to what they had to say. Folk singer Pete Seeger came to Mississippi and taught the children music, and how to play the guitar. The children's growth during this time took off and when school would arrive upon summer's end, they would find themselves way ahead of the curriculum being taught back in the segregated schools they had attended. The impact of the Freedom Schools on the black community was immeasurable.

The main effort of the project would be an increase of registered black voters. In Mississippi, it was stated by whites when confronted that blacks have always had voting rights. However, due to the efforts of the White Citizens Council, blacks were not seen as American voters, but rather black voters. Certain tactics were put into place to discourage black citizens from registering to vote. Students faced an uphill battle trying to convince citizens within the black community that attempting to register to vote was worth risking their lives over. Some people would agree to register when being talked to about it but would then decide against it when it came down to going to the courthouse. Those that were brave enough to go to the courthouse, even escorted with students and other volunteers, would turn around and walk away at the sight of a white sheriff walking around with a gun holstered to his hip. Still, there were those black citizens who were determined to have their voice heard by following the steps of registration. The effort of these citizens was thwarted by clerks and court officials by implementing "literacy tests" and impossible questions expected of them to answer. "How high can Jim jump?" "How many bubbles can a bar of soap produce?" "How many rain drops can a water puddle hold?" Black citizens were often asked to write out or interpret a selected section of the Mississippi Constitution. The slightest misspelling or any other fallacy (whatever excuse a white person could come up with) would result in denial of registration.

Another tactic implemented by whites would be direct confrontation to the voter themselves and use of intimidation. It would typically be something along these lines "Well Mr. Jones! You're not really going to register to vote, now are you? Don't you work for Mr. So and So? He wouldn't be too happy to know you were here. I sure would hate for you to lose your job over something like this. You better go on home now." This would deter any person from attempting to register, even if they were brave enough to make it to the courthouse. Poll taxes were also a major deterrent, given the majority of the black population was poor and couldn't afford to pay. The main focal point of the project would prove to be largely unsuccessful.

The efforts by volunteers and students continued despite the various ups and downs everyone would now find themselves facing. On June 20th, student volunteers sent to Mississippi included Andrew Goodman, a twenty-year-old from Queens College in New York, and twenty-four-year-old Michael Schwerner from Brooklyn. Twenty-one-year-old James Chaney, a native of Meridan, accompanied them to their first assignment near Philadelphia, MS, to the site of a church burning. The three volunteers went to investigate and were expected to check in with regular phone calls back to COFO (Council of Federated Organizations) headquarters as a precaution.

No phone call from the three men would be received. Tensions started to rise as time slowly ticked by with no word. Everyone feared the worse, and they were declared missing. The disappearance of Goodman, Chaney and Schwerner sent a wave of fear to everyone involved with the project. Word was sent to the FBI and the Justice Department, in addition to local police about the men's disappearance. Pressure was placed on Washington to send the FBI to Mississippi to investigate. Word was sent the men had been arrested by the sheriff in Neshoba County but later released. Rita Schwerner, wife to Michael, knew the chances of being released from jail and still being alive without checking in was very slim.

Rumors began to circulate with white locals that they believed the men were back in Chicago or somewhere up north, probably having a good laugh at the Mississippi folks down here. Better yet, they were maybe back in Cuba with the other "communists." If asked by reporters and media if the locals thought they might be dead, the typical response was, "Well, if they are, then they deserved it." The disappearance of the men rattled those involved with the project. Efforts continued amid the rising tensions, both on the parts of the students with their continued dedication despite the fear, and on the part of the FBI who would increase their people and the search for the missing men.

In the same month, many blacks attempted to participate in the primary election for the state, only to be found that they were not allowed to do so. Unable to vote in the election, a new political party was formed; The Mississippi Freedom Democratic Party. At the time, the state Democratic Party only allowed whites to participate, and the established system would not allow for its black citizens to vote. In fact, they had been excluded from the political system since 1890. Founding members included Ella Baker, Fannie Lou Hamer, and Bob Moses, with the chairperson being Lawrence Guyot. The hope for change was on the horizon. A lot of work was to be done before the State Convention was to be held on August

4th but hope for change was on the horizon. The Mississippi Freedom Democratic Party was the answer.

Meanwhile, the efforts of the FBI to locate the three missing volunteers resulted in uncovering several bodies and torsos unrelated to the original search. So, the search continued. One has to wonder if these bodies would have ever been found had it not been for the attention of the media due to two of the workers being white. The uncovered bodies gained no recognition and were quickly forgotten.

A victory was finally won on July 2, 1964. The Civil Rights Act was signed by President Lyndon B. Johnson with Dr. King standing beside him. However, this monumental achievement held little bearing on Mississippi as they held on to black voter suppression tactics and were determined not to allow black citizens to have their equal rights. The Jim Crow South attempted to hold on to its "way of life" by not upholding Federal Law before with the Freedom Rides and rulings before it. As William Simmons, leader of the Citizens Council stated, "Black people have had voting rights in this state all along. The Citizens Council has always taken a position that anyone who is qualified to vote should register and vote and be a good citizen." Qualifying to vote, of course, meant enforcing any tactic and strategy necessary to keep blacks from voting. Otherwise, this would lead to mass voting and more so to the advancement for black political power.

On August 4th, two days before the Mississippi Freedom Democratic Party would meet for the first time at the state convention, a tip would lead FBI agents to an earthen dame on a farm near Philadelphia, where they would uncover the bodies of Chaney, Goodman, and Schwerner. All three of the men had been shot; however, the body of James Chaney had sustained broken bones and was brutally beaten.

There was a positive spirit in the air as the delegates of the Mississippi Freedom Democratic Party arrived in Atlantic City. If there wasn't a way to bring about a change on the state level, then the possibility could be found by seeking it from the National level. The newly founded party went through the process of doing everything by the rules according to the Democratic Party. Of course, the white delegation went by none of them. Both sides would present to a credentials committee and the decision rested in their hands as to who would be chosen to represent the state of Mississippi. Mrs. Fannie Lou Hamer was chosen to speak about the goings on in Mississippi on TV. President Johnson did everything within his power to convince a determined Mrs. Hamer to not proceed with her speech in front of a live TV audience. Anyone who knew Mrs. Hamer already knew the attempt by the president would fail. As Mrs. Hamer began her speech, President Johnson implemented an impromptu press conference, where the cameras had to cut away from Ms. Hamer's speech. The urgency of this press conference from the White House? To announce the nine-month anniversary of Governor Connally was shot alongside President Kennedy. During this time, the decision came back from the credentials committee to "compromise" and give the party two seats. Dr. King told the delegates they should strongly consider taking the compromise. However, the delegates decided to turn it down. To do otherwise would be turning their back on the people back home in Mississippi.

The following year would prove to be monumental as all eyes were turned towards Selma. Of course, tensions were rising on both sides of the racial divide. The Movement had made many gains despite certain setbacks, yet there was still the looming problem of voting rights. All of the lunch-counter demonstrations, protests, boycotts, would be for not if every black American citizen was not afforded the equal opportunity to cast a vote. The white community was equally determined on the opposite end of the spectrum to not allow this to happen. To allow it would mean the downfall of every advancement they had made to dominate in society. They might have desegregated the schools, buses, terminals, etc. but the white community would be damned if they allowed a black person to cast a ballot. The Jim Crow justice would take its stand.

The little town of Selma, Alabama resided in Dallas County, which was notorious for voter exclusion of black citizens. Just like other places in the south, attempts by blacks to register to vote were met with threats, bombings, and the possibility of lynchings. The SCLC, with the invitation of Dr. King, decided to make Selma its focal point to demonstrate its tactics in making voter registration for black citizens its objective.

On January 2, 1965, the SCLC began its voter registration efforts, but the cause was met by the local sheriff and law enforcement with a violent reaction. Selma's black citizens were beaten and arrested. It's worth noting there were now more blacks filling the jail cells in the small town, then there were listed on the voter rolls. The voter registration efforts continued.

By February 18th, a number of black citizens decided to participate in a night march in Marion, Alabama, not too far outside of Selma. It was a peaceful march with no signs of resistance and was soon met with violence as troopers confronted the citizens. Jimmie Lee Jackson, while trying to protect his mother from the brutality of the troopers, was shot and killed. This would be the turning point, and only eight days after the murder, Civil Rights leader, James Bevel, called for other leaders within the movement to organize a march from Selma to Montgomery in honor of Jimmie Lee Jackson. It was decided the time to act and call for national attention would be now.

Dr. King, Bevel, and other leaders within The Movement knew the reactions expected from the law enforcement to protect blacks from voting, which meant any means necessary and would most assuredly include violence. The strategy of pairing nonviolent resistance against the brutality of the police would prove to be a tactic that would banish all doubt in the nation's mind as to the Jim Crow South's refusal to allow its black citizens the fundamental, guaranteed right to vote. It was settled. The march from Selma to Montgomery would be a call to action.

The march began on March 7th as black citizens of Selma, the surrounding areas and student activists made their way up to the Edmund Pettus Bridge. The participants of the peaceful march came to a halt as they met with troopers shouting warnings and not allowing for passage to the other side of the bridge. As the marchers advanced, the troopers came towards them; some of them on horses. As expected, one of the most violent altercations caught on film was delivered by troopers who beat the participants mercilessly with nightsticks and released teargas on them. An unconscionable type of brutality erupted, and the troopers trampled over people and beat them in a barbaric fashion. John Lewis, an original Freedom Rider who would eventually become a U.S. Senator from Georgia, was hit over the head by a trooper and suffered a fractured skull. Elderly women were beaten down in the street as they tried to escape. It was a blood-thirsty, monstrous sight that would become known as "Bloody Sunday."

The following Monday, newspapers across the world reported the violent acts that took place in Selma that Sunday. The photographs were shocking, and the strategy proved successful. Now there would be no doubt that due to the violence witnessed at Selma, there would need to be quick legislation for voter reform.

Bloody Sunday was a turning point for the Civil Rights Movement. No longer could anyone deny or overlook the injustice and horror pertaining to voting rights in the South, and the denial of it to black citizens. President Johnson addressed a joint session of Congress to persuade them of legislation that would guarantee voting rights for all. In his speech he sent out the urgent cry stating, "There is no moral issue. It is wrong, deadly wrong, to deny any of your fellow Americans the right to vote in this country. It's all of us who must overcome the crippling legacy of bigotry and injustice." And then with an echoing cry borrowed from The Movement, and displaying a stern countenance that meant business, he ended by saying, "And we SHALL overcome!"

Dr. King later joined an attempt at a second march in Selma only to be blocked again by troopers. This time things ended peacefully, as Dr. King made the decision to turn around and not allow violence to ensue. Over the next two weeks, the SCLC negotiated with federal officials to seek an injunction to prevent the State of Alabama from interfering with the march. After a federal judge ruled in their favor, the march from Selma to Montgomery began on March 21, 1965.

From start to finish, the bill passed Congress in six months and on August 6, 1965 President Johnson signed the Voting Rights Act into law, with Dr. King and other Civil Rights leaders present. This landmark piece of legislation overcame barriers on the state and local levels which would prevent blacks from exercising their right to vote. No more literacy tests, or the use of poll taxes, would be allowed and now be under investigation by the U.S. Attorney General.

Although a victory had been won, black voter turnout in Mississippi was still facing challenges. A reluctance to change and abide by federal legislation was something the South excelled at. Although literacy tests were banned, it didn't stop the continued use of fear tactics on behalf of white citizens in the state who were determined to keep blacks from voting.

      The following year, James Meredith announced he would be doing a "March Against Fear" to encourage black voter registration in his home state of Mississippi. The march would consist of starting in Memphis, Tennessee and ending in Jackson, Mississippi. It would be a total of 320 miles from start to finish. Only four years early, Meredith integrated the campus of Ole Miss. However, he found himself with very little support. By the second day into the march, shots rang out from behind a thicket of bushes and hit Meredith. A photographer happened to snap a phot of Meredith on the ground, bloody after being hit, and word reached Dr. King where he immediately left Atlanta to be with Meredith.

      It was then decided the leaders from The Movement would pick up where Meredith left off and finish the march for him. It was important to send a message of encouragement to the black community and to not complete the march would also send an unwanted message to the Citizens Council and bigots as well. The message would become, "We are not afraid, and we will continue." It was decided to keep the march locally in the south-mainly Mississippi; since the people of Mississippi would benefit the most from it.

      By the time the march reached Greenwood, Dr. King had to leave temporarily for an event in Memphis. Taking advantage of the moment and of the familiar territory where SNCC was slowly leaning more towards an advancement of blacks with the exclusion of whites, Stokely Carmichael gave a speech with Dr. King's absence and started encouraging the term "Black Power," The air of the march changed from the SCLC's peaceful and nonviolent slogan "Freedom Now" to engulf Carmichael's more aggressive black power. White participants in the march now felt their presence was unwanted. A noticeable shift in energy was immediately observed when Meredith returned to the march in Canton on June 24th. Encounters of violence had been experienced along the march, including Dr. King and others being attacked by whites and even met with clubs and nightsticks by police. However, the march did achieve its goal of registering new black voters, although it would be seen as a shift in The Movement, as Black Power would now be echoed across the country.

"Ain't gonna let nobody turn me 'round
Turn me 'round, turn me 'round
Ain't gonna let nobody turn me 'round
I'm gonna keep on a walkin', keep on a talkin'
Walkin' into Freedom Land.

"Ain't gonna let segregation turn me 'round
Turn me 'round, turn me 'round
Ain't gonna let segregation turn me 'round
I'm gonna keep on a walkin', keep on a talkin'
Walkin' into Freedom Land."

Civil Rights Movement song

"One person can make a difference."

Hezekiah Watkins

CHAPTER NINE

Passing the Torch

When I look back on my experiences, it was the young folks who were making the difference. Now, I'm too old. Most of us from The Movement are too old or have passed on and my hope is to encourage the younger folks to get involved more. I used to hear Dr. King say, "If it's not what you believe in and it's not worth dying for, you might as well be dead." I had a hard time with that. Here I was out there struggling every day- being beaten and going to jail. I knew I believed in what I was doing, but was I ready to die? The answer was no. When you think about dying, that's sad. No one wants to die. At least I don't, but we know it's coming one day. How do you prepare yourself for death? There's no way. Yet, there I was facing it. We must keep encouraging the young folks. They will be the ones to make the difference.

Throughout my experiences I've found it always takes a person on the front line to make a difference. How many of us can say that we have truly done something important in our lives that brought about a change or made a difference in some way? It doesn't mean you have to go to jail or be beaten. It doesn't take those things to make a difference. Just to be there, and to provide encouragement affects someone. The encouragement that was given to me (and all of us) then and even today, makes me feel that we were doing the right thing. It's important.

Making a difference can also be easy to begin and has the potential to catch on quickly. I was having a conversation with a young man recently about this topic. He was genuinely interested in how to get involved and try to create a change for the better. I started off by asking him a simple question; "How many friends would you say you have?

True friends, that is." He said, "Maybe five." I told him "Okay, good. If you've got five friends, can you count on them at any time of day or night? For example, if tomorrow when you go to school, you started out your day by going outside and picking up the trash on campus, do you think your five friends would come out and help if you asked?" He said, "Yes. Of course they would." "Well great!" I responded. "So how many friends do you think those five friends of yours have?" He said with a puzzled look on this face, "Maybe three or four." I said "Okay. If those three or four friends came out to help those who were already there…What do you have? You have a little movement you started. A little clean up the campus movement, and that thing can grow, you know? That's how things get done." The young man was very receptive to what I said, and it's true. That's how movements get started. That's how it was for us back in the Sixties. It's not hard to make a difference, it just requires action. Anyone can do it.

During The Movement here in Jackson, we had Medgar Evers. The NAACP wasn't pleased with a lot of things Medgar was doing. The role they were playing in other cities was actually very little (they didn't really play a part. It was all SNCC and CORE). The NAACP was there for legal guidance and that was it. We were out raising money and using this money to get out of jail and dealing with the injustices that had been handed down to someone, whether it was a Freedom Rider or whatever. The NAACP only wanted Medgar to participate in speaking engagements to raise money and to not be up front with things. Here in Jackson it wasn't like that. When Medgar began to order boycotts on different stores, based on how those stores would serve whites before blacks, a lot of times it didn't do a lot of good because people would still go to those stores, even though you were telling them not to. Then it was Medgar who decided to do a demonstration at those stores. We were fined and began to walk the sidewalks. We also began at that point to think, "You know, this guy's okay." He began to take the lead and take charge for a moment. We, the youth, thought Medgar was moving too slow in the beginning. It was at this point he began to hold different meetings throughout the community, and he had a lot of community input so we got behind what he was doing and supported him. I don't know who those Field Secretaries were in those other cities, but you didn't hear anything about the NAACP. In Jackson, it was just the opposite.

Medgar had an incredible impact on my life and to all of us who knew him. I remember one time we were at a mass meeting. A bunch of us were cuttin' up in the back of the church while Medgar was speaking. We were getting tired of the injustices that were happening to us, and we wanted to go grab our guns and go out there to handle things our own way. Medgar decided to stop his speech right then and there to address us. He looked to the back of the church and asked us a question "How many of you have guns?" Everybody in the church raised their hands, including us. "And how many of you have ammunition?" Again, everybody in the church raised their hands. We were thinking he was getting ready to tell us to go get our guns so we can shoot people, but he didn't. Instead he asked us, "If you run out of ammunition, then what are you going to do? Who's going to sell it to you? Because it's not going to be the white folks. Have you ever seen a dog chasing a car? That dog will bark and be so ferocious as the car is moving, but once that car stops, the dog doesn't know what to do. That's what would happen to us if we get out and shoot our guns and use violence. When you run out of ammunition, then you wonder what in the hell are we to do now? But then it's too late." Medgar was always preaching that violence was not going to get anywhere, and it never would. This lesson made a huge impression on me and it's something that's been with me, over the years and is still with me even today.

I think if Medgar were alive today, he would still be a believer of nonviolence. That would be the first step. During election time,, he would be into getting out there and getting people registered. He would be wanting people to vote. I think those are the things he would be concerned with today. Mainly voting. We can only hope that would be the way he would be thinking. You look at how he was such a tender man and soft-spoken. He was always reminding us of the importance of nonviolence and I feel he'd still be encouraging us all in the same manner.

Right now, the younger generation is looking for leadership. The leadership they're looking for is also right there within them. It could be someone next door- someone they go to school with. It could be someone they play with. People are looking for another Martin Luther King Jr. but there will never be another. The young folks are going to have to develop their own MLK. They're going to have to do what only they know they can do. It doesn't take a lot to make a difference. We just need one person. I don't know who that person is, but that person is out there, they just haven't surfaced yet. I look at it like boxing, or sports in general: When guys get out there on the field or on the court, they set these records. But then someone else comes along and they break those records. While that person is playing, they say, "He's the best. He's this and that. His record will probably never be broken." But those records are broken. Someone comes along just a little better, a little smarter than that person. I think the same thing is going to happen in the black community but whether or not I get a chance to see it, I don't know. But I do know there has to be someone out there who can lead. I hope I'm around long enough to see this and continue to see things move in the right direction.

I was talking with a man not long ago while at the Civil Rights Museum here in Jackson and he mentioned Dr. King talking about his dream. He asked the questions, "How many dreams are out there, and how many dreams have been fulfilled? Have they happened? Most importantly- What is the dream?" I think we've forgotten Dr. King's message and have gotten away from that. In the 60's it was just plain equality. Equal jobs.

Equal pay. Equal everything. But it's not happening now. We have so many influential blacks that straddle the fence but you don't know which way they're going or what their beliefs are. We don't have a leader at this time. It makes you wonder.

Additionally, younger folks twenty-five years and younger just don't seem to have that drive. They don't have an inkling of an idea of this road that was paved for them. They're definitely not taking advantage of it. Even the older folks, the ones that are my age (and by the way I'm 71) say they don't remember what was going on right here in Jackson. They say, "I know where the bus station is, but I don't recall riding on the back of the bus." The buses that ran in the black community did not have to go through many of the white neighborhoods, so you could sit basically wherever you wanted to because they weren't going to pick up any white passengers. These same folks also say they don't remember not eating at the restaurant they wanted to. Those are the ones who are hurting their kids and their grandkids by not letting them know how things were back then. It's a real shame too, because I definitely remember those days of having to sit at the back of the bus, drink out of the water fountain labeled "Colored," and place my order at the back window of a restaurant.

I would tell the younger folks of today to take a stand on anything that is unjust. Start a movement on something. There's a lot of injustices out there. Just do something. You can start feeding homeless folks in the park; anything that could catch on for younger people. You'd be surprised how much it could help. We didn't have social media back then. We interacted more with people. There's always something for youth these days in regards to technology; a game, video, etc… something for them to do other than what they're supposed to be doing. Young folks should be more involved in current issues.

One of the greatest opportunities I had to make a difference was when I acquired the Corner Food Market and Deli. It was a small convenience store in a bad part of Jackson. I was working for the county at the time and had a meeting at Jackson State University one day. I was running a bit late so I decided to take a shortcut. The shortcut I took led me past this little store which was close to the campus. I was smoking a cigarette and decided to go inside to buy more. The man inside the store didn't have the particular brand I wanted, so I inquired about another brand. When he didn't have that one either, I made the comment that he didn't have a big selection. The owner made the comment that it didn't do him a lot of good to carry a lot of inventory, then asked me if I had any interest in buying the store from him. The question caught me a bit off-guard, but being in a hurry I told him, "Yeah. Let's talk," as I made my way out the door and on to my meeting.

About a week or two later, I drove back to the store and went inside to talk to the man. He made me an offer. I wasn't sure at the time if it was a good offer or a bad one, so I told him no. A week later, he called me to ask if I was still interested. I told him yes and mentioned the proposition to my wife. After some discussion, I went back and struck a deal with the owner. It was for a short period of time that I would lease his store.

After several months, I began to get comfortable with the store. I added to the inventory and things started to look a bit brighter. A few more months quickly went by and before I realized it, the lease was up. I asked the owner about selling me the store rather than leasing it. We settled on a price, had the papers drawn up, and then I was off and running!

The first thing I noticed was how a lot of kids in the area were on food stamps. I wanted to do something to help the people and to make things better. After my wife gave birth to our daughter, she came up with several ways we could give back to the community. During this time, the location of the store was also a drug-infested area. We wanted to help change things, so we decided to start a community policing program. We had two police officers assigned to us in the community where the store was located. We began to do things in the community, and with the help of the police officers, a change big change happened.

Our first task was to start an enrichment program for the kids. The National Guard gave us a tent, and they even erected it for us. We invited speakers to come in and talk to the community. We would have about fifty or more kids every day. Some of the speakers would be political figures, dignitaries, radio personalities, sports figures… you name it. We also had a variety of academic curriculum for them, and we provided food for the kids as well. When we started this and it continued, it even inspired other communities to do the same with block parties that included school supply give aways. Each year we would ask the city for permission to go into the streets and in that same lot, we had Blues Artists to come in and perform from about 11 am until dark. It was wonderful!

Since it was a high crime area, we took measures to help clean it up but couldn't do it alone. We had a partnership with the Jackson Police Department and Sheriff and formed our own neighborhood watch program. If anyone witnessed any sort of crime, whether it was drug related, gambling, prostitution, or any sort of suspicious behavior, they would call me. I would then call the police department and the issues were handled immediately. It was because of this line of communication between the community, myself and the police department and all of us working together that we were able to get this area clean up for the better.

When Thanksgiving came around, we gave away turkeys. During Christmas, we made fruit baskets to deliver to the elderly. We adopted families to help. We paid light bills for those who needed the assistance. We befriended the chief of the Fire Department, and we noticed they had all of these smoke detectors that were just sitting there not being used. We were able to get every home in the community installed with a smoke detector. Whatever was needed in the community, we became what was needed.

As a result of our hard work in this community and completely turning it around for the better, I had a surprise visit from then- U.S. Attorney General under the Clinton administration, Janet Reno. She had recently been appointed and had heard about the great job we were doing in this area which was filled with drugs and crime, and wanted to personally meet the person who said, 'No more." It was one of my greatest joys to sit down and talk with her. We discussed all the ways we initiated change in the community. Ms. Reno was just as warm-hearted and down to earth as she could be. All of these good kinds of things can happen if you have the right mindset. It can catch on.

When I look back to those days, I feel it's important to share with the youth of today how everything really was. The era of the Jim Crow South left its mark on us, and it was a horrible time in our country's history. If we're not careful, we could find ourselves reliving it all over again. I look at what's happening in our country today, and some of the same old mindsets and tactics that were around back in my day are still here. It's been suppressed and is finding ways to come out without being detected. All of the tactics being used back in the day, including, "Give me the number of peas/marbles in the jar…" went underground for a while until something new could be done to suppress us. Every time you come up with a way to defeat that mindset, they come up with a way not to.

I thought things had gotten better. I really did. But I think what happened was a lot of people just suppressed their thoughts and beliefs. When a new administration came along in 2016, nothing was held back. People started thinking, "Well, since it's all out there in the open, then I can do the same thing."

We have to go back and put the Lord Jesus Christ into the equation. I'm a firm believer the hate was always there, within their minds, hearts and souls, and the current rhetoric more or less brought it to the forefront. I really thought prior to 2016, race relations were better and things had died down. When you put things on the back burner and you leave them there for so long, it just stays there. A lot of this racism and hatred was on the back burner. Then it was brought from the back to the front burner and even turned up a notch or two, causing our society to regress. Right now, we are not moving forward. Almost daily you hear of some type of hate crime that has been committed. We heard of hate crimes taking place under other administrations, but they weren't taking place as freely as they are now.

Looking at things today, I think times are actually worse now. I feel we could be looking at some sort of civil disturbance or even, I hate to go as far as to say, some sort of Civil War if we're not careful. I think to myself often, "How can all of this be? How can it be fifty plus years since The Movement, and hatred is picking up like the steam of a locomotive? However, it still comes down to this:

Racism is taught. You're not born with it. So the extremists out there, they were already halfway in the making. It didn't take much to set it off. Just like a firecracker that's lit, sometimes igniting and sometimes not. You think it's not going to ignite so you run up to it, and then all of a sudden… it blows up on you. People are just ignited with this hate and it's ready to go off at any given moment. I think a lot of it is also how children are raised. For example, the words and little things you say around them…they are going to pick up and use. With these White Supremacists, it's already in their minds and in their heads. Then the current president comes along and says a little something and they think, "Oh! I can use that… or I can say that… or I can do that." Those kinds of things can't do anything but hurt. I think they feel as though they have a voice, or a leader more or less, who allows them to say and do things that are irreparable, and get away with it. So, yes, I do think it's worse now. Even back in the Sixties, our leaders didn't preach the things that are being preached now. If it was in them, it did not surface.

In 2011, we celebrated the 50th anniversary of the Freedom Rides here in Jackson. As part of the reunion, we loaded the buses and drove to Parchman Penitentiary to take a tour where the Freedom Riders were once held. That was my first time to go back since I was there at the age of thirteen. Once we arrived, the tour guide said we were going to get off the bus and visit Death Row. I, however, got off the bus and went in another direction. Not everybody wanted to go inside the facility. I was one of those who didn't want to; however, my wife insisted so I ended up going because of her. In retrospect, I'm glad I did because it helped me by being on the outside looking in, as opposed to being on the inside as an inmate. I don't think I ever told her thank you, but because of her I was able to begin a healing process within me.

One of the things I found out by revisiting Parchman was how they don't use Death Row anymore. There's another section of the penitentiary that serves as Death Row. When they took us to the original Death Row facility, and as soon as the doors were opened and we walked in, I was the first person who made the comment the smell had not changed. There's a strong odor that's indescribable and can't be gotten rid of. The guy that was over the Correction Department, who served as our tour guide, explained to us they had spent thousands and thousands of dollars trying to get rid of the smell. A company would come in and do everything they could to make the smell go away, then a few months later it would come back. The only thing I could attribute that smell to was the number of individuals who were killed there throughout its history. It was horrible! Every person who got off the bus that day said the same identical thing.

I was also surprised to find out there was no fence around the perimeter of Parchman. Parchman was one of the most notorious prisons in these United States. They would dare inmates to break out because everything was flat land. The only thing they had was a tower. The guards would sit up in the tower and could see your every movement, and if you were inclined to escape, they would wait for hours before they put the dogs out. Once the dogs stopped barking, they would go out and gather your remains. This is what I was told when we went for the visit. That's got to be one the most horrifying things that could happen to an individual- being mauled by a dog.

Throughout my visit back at Parchman, everything began to make sense to me. The Freedom Riders were sent to Parchman because of the horrible reputation it had. I didn't know any of this when I was arrested and sent to Death Row at the age of 13. However, during that moment, standing there 50 years later, I began to understand. When I thought back to those days, I know I wasn't as brave as the other Freedom Riders were. Yet, we were all connected in our experience together, in this horrible place. It was an experience I'll never forget.

Now I spend my days passing the torch along to all who come to visit the Mississippi Civil Rights Museum, where I get to share what I've learned through my experiences. When I first went to work there, I couldn't talk about a lot of things that happened to me. Especially the part when I was in Parchman. It wasn't because the museum wouldn't allow it but because it was too hard on me to discuss. I never talked to my wife about this. She never knew anything about my experience at Parchman until recently, and I've been married to her for almost a hundred years. There are things that you block out of your mind. I think you may have heard this old saying, "Some things you'll take to your grave." That was probably going to be one of the things I was going to take to my grave. Ironically, the subject slipped out while I was talking to a group of kids at the museum. When the next group arrived, it came out again, then again. Before long, I was able to talk about it.

I feel every Freedom Rider probably suffers from PTSD - Post Traumatic Stress Disorder - and they should have been provided some type of therapy. All of them were sick through trauma. I know several that never did regain their sanity. They died not being fully productive based on what happened to them.

As I began working for the museum, I started having vivid dreams and flashbacks. Although I'm under a doctor's care now for a sleep disorder, none one of this happened until I began working there. I was seeing everything at the museum on a daily basis, and it brought back memories. Every now and then, my wife tells me I have "episodes." I had one recently where I was fighting and coming close to falling off a cliff because I was surrounded by a group of police officers. My wife will joke to make me feel better and say, "Well, I can see you fought your way out of it." Just a little humor, you know? To make it not as bad. This has happened to others as well. You don't know how bad each person has it. However, through the bad also comes the good. There is a healing process that takes place every day for me by working at the museum. Every visitor that comes through the doors is not the same. Their questions are not the same. They don't look at me the same. Some of the questions that are asked are healing to me. They ask things like, "Where do we go from here?", "What can I do?", or "I'm sorry."

Not long ago, we had a group of high school students to visit from Starkville, MS. I was proud of the speech I gave to them, and was completely satisfied with the interaction that took place that day. On the way out, there was this young white male who acted as if he wasn't in a hurry. He kept bringing up small talk. When we got out into Gallery Three of the museum, he thanked me again by saying, "Mr. Watkins, I just really thank you so very much." I said, "Okay. You're welcome." He said, "I'm going to come back again." I said, "Please do," and he walked off, but then he walked back to me and said, "Mr. Watkins…" I said, "Yes?" He said, "Can we pray?" I said, "Yes. By all means." We knelt down in Gallery Three and this young man prayed a prayer that would've healed the Devil. Now, out of all the individuals I've met… Out of all the things that's been said… That one took the cake. It wasn't a short prayer either. Even though he didn't know my family or anything, he prayed for me, everyone in my family, for him, for his family, for his school, for better race relations… He just kept on and on. People were coming through there and were watching. When we got up, tears were being wiped away. That, to me, was the most exciting time I ever had at the museum because I knew I had reached that young man, and that young man would end up impacting others. I saw the tears in their eyes. I knew he had gotten to them as well. I know at least one life was changed that day, and that's what it's all about. You've got to keep hope alive. If it dies, then you might as well be dead yourself.

Ohhhh….. Freedom.
Ohhhh…. Freedom.
Ohhhh…. Freedom, over me.
Before I'll be a slave,
I'll be buried in my grave,
And go on to my Lord
and be free.

"In the days ahead, we must not consider it unpatriotic to raise certain basic questions about our national character."

Dr. Martin Luther King Jr.

Where Do We Go from Here: Chaos or Community?

pushing FORWARD

CHAPTER TEN

Where Do We Go from Here?

One of the main questions posed by participants in the Civil Rights Movement at the end of every meeting consisted of asking the simple, yet complex question: "Where do we go from here?" The great Dr. King even titled one of his five books this very question. The answer was always pondered and mulled over by great minds, but never truly answered. At the time the book was written, a great deal of division, uncertainty, and uneasiness lay within the country. Many today ask this same question. The answer is still as obscure as it was back then.

We have all heard the old adage from Philosopher, George Santayana: "Those who cannot remember the past are condemned to repeat it." One cannot help but truly reflect on the relevance and importance of this statement and note the parallels of the issues fought for during the Civil Rights Movement and those we find ourselves confronting today. The gap of racially related issues has grown larger instead of closing in altogether. There is a continued problem of police brutality against unarmed men and women in the black community, resulting in the murder of black men all across this country. The mass incarceration of blacks remains the highest across the world. One only has to read the earlier accounts in this book to be reminded of how police brutality was in full force in our nation's past. Minorities face widespread discrimination on a daily basis and their civil liberties and rights continue to be slowly stripped away. As you're reading this, families escaping indescribable atrocities from other countries who are seeking asylum at our borders, wind up facing an additional nightmare of having their children being torn from their arms and not knowing when, or if, they will ever be reunited with their family again. In the interim, they are placed in internment camps, a lesson we should have learned from World War II and sought to never again repeat those mistakes. Why seek to reunite families, and do the right thing, when private companies are able to turn a profit from it? If those families are finally able to be reunited, then reprehensible damage is done to the children once their back with their parents and can be seen in the blank and emotionless stares, instead of affectionate hugs and tenderness. The emotional and psychological scars will remain with them their entire life.

Blatant discrimination exists in all forms and rears its ugly head in broad daylight, just like it did not so long ago, with a newfound boldness and without fear of reprimand. Hispanic men and women are shouted to return to Mexico, and chants at schools of "Build the wall" are now commonplace. If you even look to be of Hispanic origin, or speak Spanish, your culture is mocked, legal status questioned, language insulted, and immediately judged as unworthy as shouts of blatant discrimination are thrown out. Women, showing solidarity for one another and being the vocal center in the "Me Too" movement, have come forth to share their stories in a courageous manner only to find themselves being mocked and belittled, their credibility questioned and told that in this day and age we better be protecting our sons. In Georgia, members of the Black Voters Matter, a group of about 40 seniors, were not allowed to get off the bus to exercise their right to vote and were turned away; an example of modern-day voter suppression. In Mississippi, a run-off in the Senate campaign featured a candidate who made the comment of how if she were invited to attend a public hanging, she'd be in the front row. Words that she would later address as being "an exaggerated expression of regard" and would offer no apology. ICE agents, Immigration and Customs Enforcement now inspect passengers on Greyhound buses, profiling people that look "suspicious" as they ask them to step outside so they can interrogate and examine paperwork without apology. Fortunately for passengers, Greyhound has chosen to inform riders of their rights. This sure didn't happen during the Freedom Rides.

These are but just a few examples that make the adage about not repeating history revel in the mind. Are we living in the 21st century, or are we reverting to the days of Jim Crow tactics and mindsets? Or, better yet, did we ever really defeat them, or have they been thinly veiled and hiding in the shadows just waiting for the opportunity to reinvent themselves to change with the times? The comparisons and parallels are frightening.

If we fully examine and reflect on the question of determining where we go from here, it's vital that we first look to our past and study its lessons as a way of guiding us to where we need to be as an inclusive and successful society for all people. White Supremacists spawned from the end of the Civil War and have made it their mission to oppress and keep the black community in its place by not allowing them to advance on any level while preserving a "way of life." Individuals didn't have to necessarily wear hooded robes and still found a way to infiltrate their hate and suppression into all areas of society.

 The key to moving forward together into a more inclusive society has to include learning from our past no matter how difficult the task may be. For most, this is a stumbling block and one many people are not wanting or willing to acknowledge. It's much easier to sweep the past under the rug and try to look the other way. Like a wound of any kind, not allowing it to properly heal by acknowledging its existence only allows for it to get worse. Acknowledging the past and trying our best to learn the lessons it can teach us is the only way to make a step in the right direction. We cannot change the past and right all of its wrongs, however, to forget it happened would mean countless people died in vain. America is still struggling with contradictions and racial understanding. Tensions continue to build, and we cannot afford to move backwards.

 If we, as a society, truly value humanity and equality for all, we cannot help but ask ourselves the same question of, "Where do we go from here?" This time in our country's history is a pivotal moment for human rights, civil liberties, and the continuation of our democracy. The key to maintaining and preserving it lies within everyone to decide that speaking up about these issues is important enough to risk a great deal, even if it means standing alone. We must lay our differences aside and seek understanding that its because of our difference, not despite them, that make us great. That's who we are and it's who we should continue to strive to be. To quote Dr. Martin Luther King Jr., "Are we more concerned with the size, power and wealth of our society or with creating a more just society? The failure to pursue justice is not only a moral default. Without it social tensions will grow and the turbulence in the streets will persist despite disapproval or repressive action."

 The Freedom Riders and all of those during the Civil Rights Movement, such as Hezekiah Watkins, were ordinary individuals who found strength to preserve despite the overwhelming obstacles that were before them. They dared to believe in the idea that all men are created equal enough to place their lives on the line willingly, each day. The odds were greatly against them. They challenged a systematic way of life in which certain mindsets infiltrated every aspect of society with their blatant racism and hatred;

a system put into place and sustained for hundreds of years. Police brutality was at its worst. Beatings and murders were common place and only those brave few dared to go against this system of hate and fight to dismantle it. We find ourselves once again in this same familiar place of unrest. It's a different time and another battle ground, but the war still rages on. Brave souls, and common, every day people, stood in the face of danger and confronted a monstrosity of hate because the idea that all people should be given these rights was worth laying everything on the line.

    I believe we should be asking ourselves two questions today, in addition to the one Dr. King wrote about, "Are we still willing to stand up to the ever-growing amount of hatred displayed in our country today?" If the answer is yes, then, "Are we willing to do what it takes to keep 'Pushing Forward'?" We have to decide for ourselves what kind of country we want America to be. Do we really believe in the idea that ALL men are created equally and are endowed by their Creator with certain inalienable rights, that among these are Life, Liberty, and the Pursuit of Happiness? Or are those just pointless words and meaningless ramblings? If we do believe what our founding fathers wrote in our constitution, then what are we willing to do in order to protect these rights? Are we bold enough and willing to board the Greyhound buses of today's problems? Will we be courageous enough to sit at the symbolic lunch counters of our current times and seek change? Are we willing to march, protest and use our voices to speak for others and to take a stand against the injustices we experience and fight for our human rights? Or will we choose to be silent and God forbid, indifferent? I pray we choose to be Freedom Riders of today.

    How could I have ever fathomed just how much a chance encounter at a Civil Rights Museum would forever change my life? A part of my soul was hurting then, just like it still does to this day after witnessing so many disheartening events take place in our country. I found out that day that even through the most devastating of events, there can be a healing and restoration found in our connection with others. It's people who make the difference. Hope shown through the brokenness as a beacon of light that day. I knew instantly after I met Mr. Hezekiah Watkins, that a connection was established that superseded any kind of "way of life" my white ancestors long ago fought so hard to maintain. A 71 year old black gentleman from Mississippi, who had experienced the very worst side of human beings-and had the wounds and stories to prove it- and a white woman, also from Mississippi, with an eagerness to learn, struck up a conversation that day. Two human beings stood there engaged in deep dialogue. One willing to share a story and an eagerness to pass along the lessons learned. The other willing to listen, ask questions, and wanting to understand. There was a time in Mr. Watkins' life where this type of interaction, yet alone, collaboration, would never have taken place. Yet, the result lies here in this book along with the close bond of friendship formed that no person or society could dictate. When I think about how far we have come to make changes like this possible, I can't help but also feel hopeful that the commonality of humanity and love for mankind will always triumph over hate.

The stakes are high. They were back then, and they are still today. There are those courageous few, such as the Freedom Riders, who helped to pave the way. They were young and full of idealistic enthusiasm; determined to make a difference for the better. It didn't come without a high price to pay. Many of these heroes who suffered then still carry the battle scars of a fight that continues today. Their lessons, if we are wise enough to learn from them, are there for us all. The torch is being passed from one generation of ordinary heroes to another. It's up to all of us to decide if we are willing to take it and run with it, igniting the way once paved by those before us. Will we allow it to be extinguished? Are we willing to have the constructive conversations and challenging dialogues with one another? History has shown us what could happen if we travel back down the path towards darkness. We must keep lighting the way for all and keep ***pushing forward*** together.

> *"You must be the change you wish to see in the world."*
>
> Mahatma Gandhi

pushing *FORWARD*

Hezekiah Watkins

Mr. Hezekiah Watkins was born in Milwaukee, Wisconsin but is a lifelong resident of Jackson, Mississippi where he resides today with his loving wife, Chris. He is the proud father of Marvin Lilley, Quentin Ramon, Kristi, and Shemika. He is also the doting grandfather of Corey, Brandon, Quentin II "Mook", Mason, and a great-grandfather to Kaidin and Amora Rose.

Upon graduating from Lanier High School, Hezekiah attended Utica Junior College, the University of Southern Illinois in Carbondale, Illinois and East Tennessee State at Johnson City, Tennessee and is a Vietnam War Veteran. After timed served in the Armed Forces, Hezekiah worked at the Jackson Hinds Comprehensive Health Center and was owner of the Corner Food Market and Deli in Jackson.

Aside from being known as "Mississippi's Youngest Freedom Rider" at the age of 13, Mr. Watkins has dedicated his life to pursuing justice and can be found at the Mississippi Civil Rights Museum, continuing to teach the importance of learning from history and to share his story with all who visit.

pushing FORWARD

Andrea Ledwell

Andrea Ledwell was born and raised in Mississippi. She is a graduate of Mississippi State University where she received her BS degree in Education. After years of teaching, Andrea decided to switch gears and became the Assistant Publisher for OutdoorX4 Magazine where she is a published journalist and contributing author. In 2016, Andrea received the "Excellence in Craft" award by the Texas Auto Writers Association for her article titled "Chihuahuan Adventures" about hiking the South Rim of the Big Bend region in Texas.

When not busy writing, Andrea loves to spend her time with her husband Frank and three daughters; Avery, Mallory, and Abigail. You can also find her going on adventures with her family and English Bulldog, Maggie, and exploring throughout Texas and the U.S. Although she now resides in Houston, Texas, the people and storytelling from her home state of Mississippi have been the inspiration behind much of her writing and are never far from her heart.

Acknowledgments

In the collaboration of this book, a wonderful friendship was formed over many interviews, phone calls, and visits. We would first and foremost like to thank God for allowing this friendship to take place and for the idea of making this book possible. We would also like to thank both of our families for their patience, support, and love as we worked to make this book a reality. We would like to express a great amount of appreciation for all Civil Rights activists and leaders, especially James Bevel and James Farmer, whose endless work for equality continue to inspire and influence people today. None of this could have been possible without them. Many thanks to the Mississippi Department of Archives and History and to the Mississippi Civil Rights Museum, whose efforts continue to educate future generations.

Notes

Who Are These Freedom Riders?

- Farmer, James. Lay Bare the Heart: An Autobiography of the Civil Rights Movement. New York: Arbor House, 1985.
- Nelson Jr., Stanley, producer and director. "American Experience Films: The Freedom Riders." 2010
- Voth, Ben. James Farmer Jr.: The Great Debater Lexington Books 2017

The Buses Are A-Comin'

- Tyson, Timothy B. The Blood of Emmett Till. New York: Simon & Schuster Paperbacks, 2017.
- Mississippi State Sovereignty Commission Files, courtesy of the Mississippi Department of Archives and History.
- Video, "The Children Shall Lead," William Winter Institute for Racial Reconciliation at Ole Miss
- Arsenault, Ray. Freedom Riders: 1961 and the Struggle for Racial Justice (Pivotal Moments in American History. Oxford University Press. 2007.

A Call To Action in Jackson

- Meredith, James. Three Years in Mississippi. Bloomington: Indiana University Press, 1966.
- nvdatabase.swarthmore.edu
- www.crmvet.org
- Mississippi Department of Archives and History Pursuing Equality
- Cagin, Seth and Philip Dray. We Are Not Afraid: The Story of Goodman, Schwerner, and Chaney and the Civil Rights Campaign for Mississippi. New York: Macmillan, 1988.
- King, Martin Luther, Jr. Where Do We Go From Here: Chaos or Community? Boston: Beacon Press, 1967.
- American Experience, documentary, PBS
- "The Search in Mississippi" by CBSN, 1964, narrated by Walter Cronkite
- Fayer, Steve and Henry Hampton. Voices of Freedom New York: Bantom Books, 1990

pushing FORWARD

Photographs:

- SCRID# 2-55-5-76-1-1-1: Mississippi State Sovereignty Commission, "Greyhound bus terminal sit-in mug shot," July 7, 1961, Mississippi State Sovereignty Commission Records Online, 1994-2006, Mississippi Department of Archives and History.

- SCRID# 2-55-5-74-1-1-1: Mississippi State Sovereignty Commission, "Sit-Ins- Group Number Twenty-Four" July 14, 1961, Mississippi State Sovereignty Commission Records Online, 1994-2006, Mississippi Department of Archives and History.

- SCRID# 2-140-3-45-1-1-1: Mississippi State Sovereignty Commission, article, Jackson Daily, "Negroes Hear Preacher, Six More Jailed" July 7, 1961, Mississippi State Sovereignty Commission Records Online, 1994-2006, Mississippi Department of Archives and History.

- SCRID# 2-55-5-76-2-1-1: Mississippi State Sovereignty Commission, article, "Index Card File" July 7, 1961, Mississippi State Sovereignty Commission Records Online, 1994-2006, Mississippi Department of Archives and History.